Understanding Development in Relation to Environment:
Coping Measures

Mohinder Slariya, Ph.D.
&
Dai-Yeun-Jeong

Preface and Acknowledgements

Nature has created everything in perfect manner and sustaining lives of all living creatures including human being on this planet since ages. Bedause of nurture capapcity of nature, it is known as *Mother Nature,* and since the inception of civilization, human being has been altering *Mother Nature* to make their life more comfortable and in this process of accumulation of wealth he tried to mastry over it which resulted in the deterioration in the existing set-up of society. This exploitative perspective *(dristi)* to see the creation *(sristi)* of nature has been shifted because of the change in the perspective after industrial revolution. To make human life more comfortable man has made considerable intervention in nature which was earlier not so problematic, but with the introduction of modern technologies the condition start deteriotating and today we reached at alarming stage from where it may be different to restore it. The ecological web created by the *Almighty* has been disturbed in the name of development and ill-planning which is reflecting in many natural occurances like; untime rain or no rain, extreme hot, severe cold, extreme rise and fall in temperature, increase in greenhouse gases and above all adverse impacts of climate change, which is reality now!

To understand this changing relationship and issues and challenges associated with it, three days academic venture has been planned and executed in form of international conference on *Biodiversity, Development and Climate Change: Issues and Challenges* popularly known as *Chamba Climate Meet-2014* which has been attended by numerous scholars coming from different parts of globe. The academic contributions made by them has been document in form of series *Advance in Environmental Sociology* and this is the IVth volume in a row.

Whole volume has been divided in 15 chapters focusing on different aspects. The first chapter is a review of today's one of the emerging need i.e. green chemistry by Ravdeep Saini while second chapter concenterate on threatetening medicinal plants of Rajasthan in which Krishnendra Singh Nama is advocating conservational strategy in context of climate change. The third chapter has been contributed by Kiran Chaudhary on conservation of herbal remedies for neural disorder disorders which is a case study of Mukundata hills national park in Rajasthan. The next chapter has been contributed by Manpreet Kaur and the focus of the chapter is the problem of air pollution and introduction of new index and antioxidant activities in the vicinity of cement plant based development, which could be an eye opener to the policy makers as well as executors. Anju Sehgal, an associate professor has contributed chapter on conservation issue of biodiversity and sustainable use of medicial plants.

Sixth chapter is a description of achievements of Govt. of Punjab, Pakistan for prevention and control of dengue as an outcome of unplanned development by using though standard operating procedures. The seventh chapter is an collaborative effort of research scholars and their professor to high light health issues in the state of Himachal Pradesh. Chapter VIII, IX, X, XI and XII are based on laboratory and experimental methods used by the research scholars of medical college with an advocacy for bioremedial, phytoremedial, therapetutic and antioxidant impact evaluation of arsenic induced toxicity. Chapter XIII contributed by Oinam Sunanda Devi is research based description of conservational issues related to water birds loktak lake at ramsar site. Second last chapter an effort of the Md. Abul Kalam Azad to describe efficacy of Bangladesh botanical extracts for controlling of pests in brinjal field. And the last chapter is a detailed description of shirui kashong biodiversity conservation for sustainable development has been contributed by Ninghorla Zimik.

I am thankful all the contributors of this volume and for adding their intellectual contribution in this series on *Advances in Environmental Sociology* in general and to this volume specifically. I am also thankful to co-author for giving me free hand during and after conference. I am thankful to all my students, my family and all who contributed directly or indirectly to make this volume happened. I will be happy to respond to any quarry and feedback at mkslariya@gmail.com

Place: Chamba
Date: 10.12.2015   (Dr. Mohinder K. Slariya)

Table of Content

Chapter I

Green Chemistry: Fundamental Principles and Application for Sustainable Development: A Review

Ravdeep Saini*

Abstract

"Green Chemistry" is the universally accepted term to describe the movement towards more environmentally acceptable chemical processes and products. Green chemistry, as the name implies, is part of the "greening" of corporate practices that has monoliths like Wal-Mart Stores, Inc., touting "earth-friendly" products. Over the course of the past decade, green chemistry has demonstrated how fundamental scientific methodologies can protect human health and the environment in an economically beneficial manner. In the words of Paul Anastas, who introduced the term 'green chemistry' in 1991, "It's more effective, it's more efficient, it's more elegant, and it's simply better chemistry". Significant progress is being made in several key research areas, such as catalysis, the design of safer chemicals and environmentally benign solvents, and the development of renewable feed stocks. It is an approach to product manufacturing that seeks to reduce or eliminate the use or generation of hazardous substances in the design, manufacture, and application of chemical products. The concept of green chemistry incorporates a new approach to the synthesis, processing and application of chemical substances in such manner as to reduce threats to health and environment. Current and future chemists are being trained to design products and processes with an increased awareness for environmental impact. This article presents applications of green chemistry in everyday life.

Key words: Green Chemistry, Sustainability, Hazardous chemicals, Health

*Research Scholar, Mewar University, Chittorgarh, Rajasthan

Introduction

The term "green chemistry," also known as clean chemistry or benign and sustainable chemistry, refers to the design of chemicals and formulation of processes that reduce the risk to humans and minimize environment pollution. The goal of green chemistry solutions is to lessen or eliminate hazardous impacts of chemicals over a chemical product's life-cycle. "Green Chemistry" is the universally accepted term to describe the movement towards more environmentally acceptable chemical processes and products (1). It encompasses education, research, and commercial application across the entire supply chain for chemicals (2). Green Chemistry can be achieved by applying environmentally friendly technologies – some old and some new (3). While Green Chemistry is widely accepted as an essential development in the way that we practice chemistry, and is vital to sustainable development, its application is fragmented and represents only a small fraction of actual chemistry. It is also important to realize that Green Chemistry is not something that is only taken seriously in the developed countries. Some of the pioneering research in the area in the 1980s was indeed carried out in developed countries including the UK, France, and Japan, but by the time the United States Environmental Protection Agency (US EPA) coined the term "Green Chemistry" in the 1990s, there were good examples of relevant research and some industrial application in many other countries including India and China (4). The idea of green chemistry was initially developed as a response to the Pollution Prevention Act of 1990, which declared that U.S. national policy should eliminate pollution by improved design (including cost-effective changes in products, processes, use of raw materials, and recycling) instead of treatment and disposal.

The Americans launched the high profile Presidential Green Chemistry Awards in the mid-1990s and effectively disclosed some excellent case studies covering products and processes (5). In 1996 the working party on green chemistry was created, acting within the framework of International Union of Pure and Applied Chemistry. One year later the Green Chemistry Institute (GCI) was formed with chapters in 20 countries to facilitate contact between governmental agencies and industrial corporations with universities and research institutes to design and implement new technologies. The first conference highlighting green chemistry was held in Washington in 1997. Since that time other scientific conferences have been soon held on a regular basis. The first book and journals on the subject of green chemistry were introduced in 1990, including the *Journal of Clean Processes and Green Chemistry,* sponsored by the Royal Society of Chemistry. The concept of green chemistry incorporates a new approach (6-11) to the synthesis, processing and application of chemical substances in such manner as to reduce threats to health and environment.

The 12 Principles of Green Chemistry were proposed by Anastas and Warner (12) and published in 1998, by providing the new field with a clear set of guidelines for further development. In 1999, the Royal Society of Chemistry launched its journal *GREEN CHEMISTRY.* In the last 10 years, national networks have proliferated, special issues devoted to green chemistry have appeared in major journals, and green chemistry concepts have continued to gain traction. A clear sign of this was provided by the citation for the 2005 Nobel Prize for Chemistry awarded to Chauvin, Grubbs, and Schrock, which commended their work as "a great step forward for green chemistry"(13).

Basic Principles of Green Chemistry

Prevention
It is to prevent waste than to treat or clean up waste after it has been created.

Atom Economy
Synthetic methods should be designed to maximize the incorporation of all materials used in the process into the final product.

Less Hazardous Chemical Synthesis
Whenever practicable synthetic methods should be designed to use and generate substances that possess little or no toxicity to human health and the environment.

Designing Safer Chemicals
Chemical products should be designed to affect their desired function while minimizing toxicity.

Safer Solvents and Auxiliary
The use of auxiliary substances should be made unnecessary wherever possible.

Design for Energy Efficiency
Energy requirements of chemical processes should be recognized for their environmental and at low temperature and pressure.

Use of Renewable Feedstocks
A raw material or feedstock should be renewable rather than depleting whenever technically and practicable.

Reduce Derivatives
Unnecessary derivatization (use of blocking groups, protection, and deprotection) should be avoided whenever possible.

Catalysis
Catalytic reagents (as selective as possible) are superior stoichiometric reagents.

Design for Degradation
Chemical products should be designed so that at the end of their function they break down into innocuous degradation products and do not persist in the environment.

Real-time analysis for pollution prevention
Analytical methodologies need to be further developed to allow for real-time, in process monitoring and control prior to the formation of hazardous substances.

Inherently Safer Chemistry for Accident prevention
Substances and the form of a substance used in a chemical process should be chosen to minimize the potential for chemical accidents, including releases, explosions and fires.

Green Chemistry has been promoted worldwide by an increasing but still small number of dedicated individuals and through the activities of some key organizations. These include the Green Chemistry Network (GCN; established in the UK in 1998 and now with about one thousand members worldwide) (14) Green Chemistry Networks or other focal points for national or regional activities exist in other countries including Italy, Japan, Greece and Portugal and new ones appear every year. The GCN was established to help promote and encourage the application of Green Chemistry in all areas where chemistry plays a significant role. (Fig. 1.)

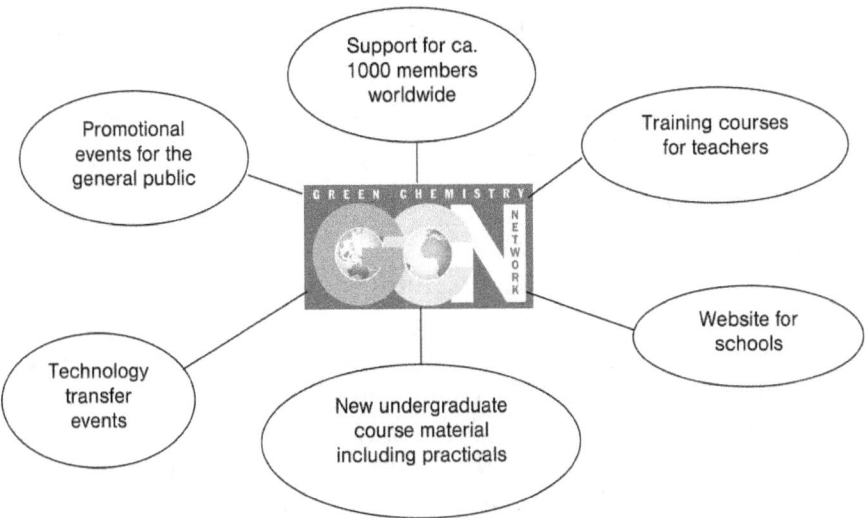

Applications of Green Chemistry

Green Chemistry in Polymer Chemistry

In the polymer area, there is also increasing interest in green chemistry. This is evident by many recent symposia organized on this topic at national ACS meetings. In our view, developments in green polymer chemistry can be roughly grouped into the following eight related themes. These eight themes also agree well with most of the themes described in recent articles and books on green chemistry (15-18).

- Greener catalysts (e.g., biocatalysts such as enzymes and whole cells)
- Diverse feedstock base (especially agricultural products and bio based building blocks)
- Degradable polymers and waste minimization
- Recycling of polymer products and catalysts (e.g., biological recycling)
- Energy generation or minimization of use
- Optimal molecular design and activity
- Benign solvents (e.g., water, ionic liquids, or reactions without solvents)
- Improved syntheses and processes (e.g., atom economy, reaction
- Efficiency, toxicity reduction)

Green Chemistry in Nanotechnology (19)

Nanotechnology is an emerging field. It is an interdisciplinary science whose potential has been widely touted for well over a decade. Despite significant private and public investment, progress moving nonmaterial's from the laboratory to industrial production has been slow and difficult. Two challenges that have slowed development have been the poor understanding of the new hazards introduced by nanotechnology and lack of appropriate policies to manage any new risks. Scientists, engineers and entrepreneurs, however, continue to move forward, grappling with challenges that range from the technical to the regulatory and everywhere in between.

Just as the concepts of nanoscale invention have required new insights from scientists, they are also demanding new approaches to managing, producing, funding and deploying novel technologies into the larger chemical sector. In this case, there is an unusual opportunity to use science, engineering and policy knowledge to design novel products that are benign as possible to human and environment health. Recognition of this opportunity has led to the development of the "green nanoscience" concept.

The project on emerging nanotechnologies at the Wood row Wilson International center for scholars launched a green nano program on Feb 2006. This initiative aims to advance the development of clean technologies of using nanotechnology to minimize potential environmental and human health risk associated with the manufacture and the use of nanotechnology products in general to apply a nano to solve legacy environmental problems and to encourage the replacement of existing products with a new nano products that are more environmentally friendly throughout their life cycle.

Green Chemistry in Education (20)

The idea of including Green Chemistry in chemistry education was first put forward in 1994. A complete course was described shortly thereafter (Collins, 1995). Few Green chemistry textbooks have also been published (Ahluwalia and Kidwai, 2003). Graduates, post graduates, teachers and researchers will find these books of immense use. Both Environmental Protection Agency (EPA) and American Chemical Agency (ACS) have recognized the importance of bringing Green Chemistry to the class room and the laboratory.

Several green chemistry activities were designed and incorporated throughout the one year organic chemistry curriculum (both lecture and lab). All activities are based on the twelve principles of green chemistry. Existing organic reactions at Chandler-Gilbert Community College (CGCC) were replaced with greener alternatives in the form of greener reagents, greener solvents, and greener methodologies. As a result of this endeavor, the generation of hazardous waste has been entirely eliminated. The green lab experiments performed during 2006–2007 academic year are listed in Table 1.

Table 1: Green Laboratory Experiments

Green Reaction	What was green in this Experiment?	Green Chemistry principle utilized
Diels-Alder Reaction at 0°C	Low temperature 0° to room temperature	1, 6, 12
Reaction 'on water'	Safer solvent system (water	1, 5, 12
Synthesis of Cyclohexene from Cyclohexanol	Solvent less condition	1, 5, 9, 12
Bromination Reactions	Bromine generated in situ; very low temperature Conditions	1,3, 6, 10, 12
Acetylation of Ferrocene	Solvent less condition; reaction performed under ambient conditions	1, 5, 6, 12
Iodination of Vanillin	Natural sources as starting material	1, 7, 12
Grignard Synthesis at low temperature	Very mild conditions	1, 6, 12
Grignard Reaction in water	Safer solvent conditions	1, 5, 6, 12
Green Oxidation	Greener oxidation conditions; water as the solvent; low temperature reactions	1, 5, 6, 8,10,12
Combinatorial Synthesis	Single step reaction to produce many products	2, 4, 6, 8

Student involvement in Green Chemistry principles and practices is essential to the integration the environmentally benign technologies in academia and industry. Suggestions for these activities include:

1. Hosting a Green Chemistry speaker
2. Organizing an interdisciplinary Green Chemistry workshop on campus
3. Working with a local company on a Green Chemistry project
4. Developing a Green Chemistry activity with a local school
5. Converting a current laboratory experiment into a greener one
6. Organizing a Green Chemistry poster sessions on campus
7. Distributing a Green Chemistry Newsletter to the local community
8. Designing a green Chemistry web page

Green Chemistry in Agriculture (21)

Green chemistry and sustainable agriculture are both revolutionary fields with significant overlap, though the connections are not fully developed nor appreciated. Sustainable agriculture encompasses a wide variety of farming techniques and practitioners. Broadly speaking sustainable agriculture seeks to achieve three goals: farm profitability; community prosperity; and environmental stewardship. The latter includes: protecting and improving soil quality, reducing dependence on non-renewable resources, such as fuel, synthetic fertilizers and pesticides and minimizing adverse impacts on safety, wildlife, water quality, and other environmental resources.

Green chemistry and sustainable agriculture are inherently intertwined; farmers need green chemists to make safe agricultural chemical inputs. Green chemists need farmers practicing sustainable agriculture to provide truly "green" bio-based raw materials to process into new products.

Biopesticides are a set of tools and applications that will help our farmer's transition away from highly toxic conventional chemical pesticides into an era of truly sustainable agriculture. Of course biopesticides are only a part of a larger solution; sustainable agriculture is a broad and deep field. But helping farmers move from their current chemical dependency to organic agriculture and beyond requires tools for the transition and tools for a new era. Biopesticides can and will play a significant role in this process.

Green Chemistry in Engineering:

In fact - Green Engineering is the process and design of products aiming to conserve natural resources leading to sustainability goals. Also, green engineering aims to reduce the impact of processes and products to the natural environment. The term —green engineering is applied to a variety of products, like houses, vehicles, consumer products (materials, electrical and electronic equipment) and devices that requires engineering technologies in the construction or making. Green engineers can now graduate from various university engineering departments in developed industrialized countries. Other engineering graduates can have special training on various fields, attending special classes to understand how materials and other components can be made in an environmentally-friendly way. For example, engineers and architects concerned with home design may learn about the latest building materials and techniques. Green engineering and design is nowadays an important additional qualification for every aspect of engineering.

Green engineering concentrates on how to promote sustainability through science and technology. Green engineers are engaged in designing new materials, products, processes and systems. There are many good examples of electrical machines and electronic products that have end-of-life design features so that can be disassembled into components, recycled, or reused with maintenance and easy repair. Xerox printers are designed so that after their commercial use, can be converted and be remanufactured. Various other big industrial companies have introduced green engineering design features in their products for easy repairs, recyclability or reuse after maintenance ((AT&T, General Electric, IBM, Procter & Gable, Whirlpool, etc). (22-24)

In the last decade there is a major shift in the way industrial manufacturers have changed the design of their products in order to reduce the end-of-life burdens to the environment. The Product Life

Cycle (PLC) analysis has become a standard method following the various stages of a product's life. From starting materials, manufacture and final disposition the life of a product is analysed quantitatively from its environmental impact and natural resources use. It is represented with a cycle: Design—Manufacturing—Distribution—Customer—End-of-Life. Many software programmes have been developed recently dealing with PLC. The PLC is associated with engineering tasks, materials and energy, but also can involve marketing activities and new product development. (25-26)

Figure 2

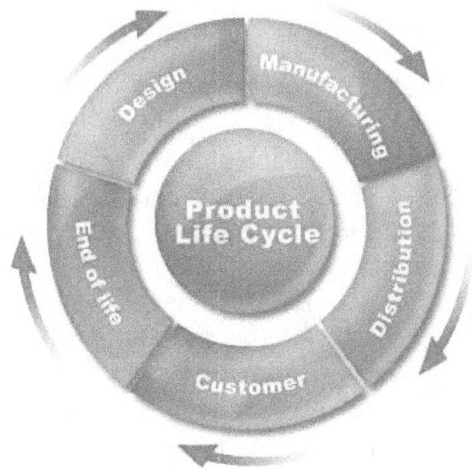

Green Chemistry in Pharmaceutical industry:

Chemistry is an integral part of our pharmaceutical business. Green chemistry is understood to be superior innovative chemistry that is cost effective and has minimal impact on the environment. Over the past decade, the pharmaceutical industry has been moving toward the application of green chemistry principles, mainly by introducing new production and analytical technologies, using greener solvents and emphasizing enzymatic chemistry.

Green chemistry focuses on making industrial chemistry safer, cleaner and more energy efficient while generating economic benefits. This concept is driven by efficiency combined with environmental responsibility to offer enhanced chemical process economics. To decrease the environmental footprint and costs associated with the production of clopidogrel hydrogen sulfate (trade name Plavix® or Iscover®), Sanofi set up an ongoing green chemistry project that has led to improved synthetic pathways, increased yields and smaller quantities of solvents in the manufacturing process. These important improvements meet the expectations of both internal and external stakeholders. The discovery of green and sustainable synthesis methodologies is a long-term endeavor. Today, collaborations between academia and pharmaceutical companies provide an opportunity to develop green, safe and more effective processes to deliver medicines for the 21st century.

New Challenges of Green Chemistry

The challenge for chemists and others is to develop new products, processes and services that achieve the societal, economic and environmental benefits that are now required. This requires a new approach which sets out to reduce the materials and energy intensity of chemical processes and products, minimize or eliminate the dispersion of harmful chemicals in the environment, maximize the use of renewable resources and extend the durability and recyclability of products—in a way which increases industrial competitiveness. Some of the challenges for chemists include the discovery and development of new synthetic pathways using alternative feedstocks or more selective chemistry, identifying alternative reaction conditions and solvents for improved selectivity and energy minimization and designing less toxic and inherently safer chemicals.

In chemical synthesis, the ideal will be a combination of a number of environmental, health and safety, and economic targets (Fig. 3).

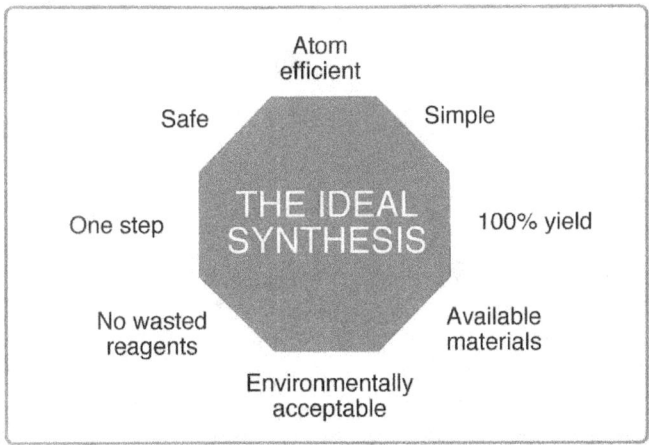

To help illustrate the many challenges ahead and the opportunities for new greener chemistry, two very broadly based generic areas of chemistry can be at least superficially examined in terms of their scope, the environmental unacceptability and poor atom economics of typical processes, and the goals and possible approaches of green chemistry. The emphasis will be on batch type processes involving liquid phase reactions as practiced by fine, specialty chemical and chemical intermediate manufacturers around the world.

Acid catalyzed reactions

Acid catalysis is the most widely used type of catalysis with applications in all sectors of the chemical, pharmaceutical and allied industries, although the largest scale use is in the petrochemical industries where the processes are largely quite efficient and the use of solid acids is well established (27)

Traditionally most liquid phase organic reactions have been catalyzed by strong Brønsted acids such as H_2SO_4 and HF and by soluble Lewis acids such as $AlCl_3$ and BF_3. These acids have many important advantages—they are cheap, readily available and very active. Unfortunately, they also suffer from some serious disadvantages, which are becoming increasingly prominent in these environmentally conscious days—they are difficult to separate from the organic products and their use leads to large volumes of hazardous waste.

Uses of Green Chemistry in daily life

Dry Cleaning of Cloths

Green Dry Cleaning of Clothes

Perchloroethylene (PERC), $Cl_2C=CCl_2$ is commonly being used as a solvent for dry cleaning. It is now known that PERC contaminates ground water and is a suspected carcinogen. A technology, known as Micell technology 1999 developed by Joseph De Simons, Timothy Romark, and James McClain made use of liquid CO_2 and a surfactant for dry cleaning clothes, thereby replacing PERC. Dry cleaning machines have now been developed using this technique. Micell Technology (28) has also evolved a metal cleaning system that uses CO2 and a surfactant thereby eliminating the need of halogenated solvents (29).

Versatile Bleaching Agents

It is common knowledge that paper is manufactured from wood (which contains about 70% polysaccharides and about 30% lignin). For good quality paper, the lignin must be completely removed. Initially, lignin is removed by placing small chipped pieces wood into a bath of sodium hydroxide (NaOH) and sodium sulphide (Na_2S). By this process about 80-90% of lignin is decomposed. The remaining lignin was so far removed through reaction with chlorine gas (Cl_2). The use of chlorine removes all the lignin (to give good quality white paper) but causes environmental problems. Chlorine also reacts with aromatic rings of the lignin to produce dioxins, such as 2, 3, 4 -tetrachloropdioxin and chlorinated furans. These compounds are potential carcinogens and cause other health problems.

These halogenated products find their way into the food chain and finally into products, pork, beef and fish. In view of this, use of chlorine has been discouraged. Subsequently, chlorine dioxide was used. Other bleaching agents like hydrogen per oxide (H_2O_2), ozone (O_3) or oxygen (O_2) also did not give this the desired results. A versatile agent has been developed by Terrence Collins of Carnegie Mellon University. It involves the use of H_2O_2 as a bleaching agent in the presence of some activators known as TAML activators[10] that as catalysts which promote the conversion of H_2O_2 into hydroxyl radicals that are involved in oxidation (bleaching). The catalytic of TAML activators allow H_2O_2 to break down more lignin in a shorter time and at much lower temperature. These bleaching agents find use in laundry and results in lesser use of water. (30)

Green Solution to Turn Turbid Water Clear

Tamarind seed kernel powder, discarded as agriculture waste, is an effective agent to make municipal and industrial waste water clear. The present practice is to use Al-salt to treat such water. It has been found that alum increases toxic ions in treated water and could cause diseases like Alzheimer's. On the other hand kernel powder is not-toxic and is biodegradable and cost effective. For the study, four flocculants namely tamarind seed kernel powder, mix of the powder and starch, starch ad alum were employed. Flocculants with slurries were prepared by mixing measured amount of clay and water. The result showed aggregation of the powder and suspended particles were more porous and allowed water to ooze out and become compact more easily and formed larger volume of clear water. Starch flocks on the other hand were found to be light weight and less porous and therefore didn't allow water to pass through it easily. The study establishes the powder's potential as an economic flocculants with performance close more established flocculants such as K2SO4Al2 (SO4) 3.24H2O (potash alum).

Conclusion

"Green chemistry offers many promises, including substantial reductions in the environmental footprint of many chemical processes, improvements in the health and safety of those exposed to chemicals, and enhanced security at facilities with hazardous materials." Green chemistry technologies can contribute to a sustainable economy, relieving the economic pressures on state and local governments, improving the profitability of businesses using safer materials, providing job opportunities, and protecting human health and the environment. Employing the twelve principles of Green Chemistry, biopesticides could provide a new generation of agricultural pest management products that are sustainable both from an environmental and health perspective.

Furthermore, the success of green chemistry depends on the training and education of a new generation of chemists. Students at all levels have to be introduced to the philosophy and practice of green chemistry. Most importantly we need the relevant scientific, engineering, educational and other communities to work together for sustainable future through Green Chemistry. Great efforts are still undertaken to design an ideal process that start from non-polluting materials.

References:

1 World Commission on the Environment and Development (WCED), Our Common Future Oxford, Oxford University Press, 1987, p. 43.
2 Quality of Life Counts: Indicators for a Strategy for Sustainable Development in the UK 2004 Update, Department for Environment, Food and Rural Affairs, London, March 2004.
3 Bjørn Lomborg, The Skeptical Environmentalist, Measuring the Real State of the World Cambridge University Press, Cambridge, 2001.
4 Ali M. El-Agraa, The European Union: Economics and Policies, 7th edition, Prentice Hall Financial Times, 2004.
5 Richard G. Lipsey, K. Alec Crystal, Economics, 10th edition, Oxford University Press, Oxford, 2004.
6. P.T. Anastas, I.T. Hovarsth, Innovations and Green Chemistry, Chem.Rev.107, 2169 (2007).
7 S. Ravichandran, Int. J. ChemTech Res., 2(4)2191 (2010).
8. B. M. Trost, Atom economy-A challenge for organic synthesis: Homogeneous catalysis leads the way. Angew Chem Int ., Ed., 34, 259 (1995).
9. R.A. Sheldon, Green solvents for sustainable organic synthesis: State of the art. Green Chem., 7, 267 (2005).
10. V.B. Bharati, Resonance, 1041 (2008).
11. V.K. Ahluwalia and M. Kidwai, New Trends in Green Chemistry, Anamaya Publisher, New Delhi (2004).

12. P.T. Anastas, J.C.Warner, Green Chem Theory and Practice, Oxford Univ. Press, Newyork (1998)
13. Development: An Environmental Technologies Action Plan for the European Union, Com (2004) 38 final, Brussels, 28 January 2004.
15. Horvath, I. T.; Anastas, P. T. Chem. Rev. 2007, 107, 2169–2173.
16. Stevens, F. S. Green Plastics: An Introduction to the New Science of Biodegradable Plastics; Princeton University Press: Princeton, NJ, 2002.
17. Lancaster, M. Green Chemistry: An Introductory Text; Royal Society of Chemistry: Cambridge, U.K., 2002.
18. Matlack, A. S. Introduction to Green Chemistry; Marcel Dekker: New York, NY, 2001
21. Green Chemistry and Sustainable Agriculture: The Role of Biopesticides Karen Peabody O'Brien, Shari Franjevic and Julie Jones Advancing Green Chemistry September, 2009
22. Boks C, Stevels A. Essential perspectives for design for environment. Experiences from the electronics industry. J Prod Res 45(18-19): 4021-4039, 2007.
23. Garcia-Serna J, Perez-Barrigon L, Cocero MJ. New trends for design towards sustainability in chemical engineering: Green engineering. Review. Chem Engin J 133(1-3): 7-30, 2007.
24. Oakley BT. Total quality product design-How to integrate environmental criteria into the product realization process. Environ Quality Manag 2(3): 309-321, 1993.
25. Brink G-JT, Avends IWCE, Sheldon RA. Green, catalytic oxidation of alcohols in water. Science 287: 1636-1639, 2000.
26. Srivastava SK. Green supply-chain management: A state-of-the-art literature review. Int J Manag Rev 9(1):53-80, 2007.
27. See for example: J. M. Thomas and W. J. Thomas, Heterogeneous Catalysis, VCH, Weinheim, 1997
28. Micell Technology, Website: www.micell.com, accessed Dec. 1999.
29. P.T Anastas and T.C.Williamson, Green Chemistry: Frontiers in Benign chemical Synthesis and Processes. Oxford University Press, Oxford. (1998).
30. 11. P. Tundo and P.T. Anastas, Green Chemistry: Challenging Perspectives, Oxford University Press, Oxford. (1998).

Chapter-II

Threatened Medicinal Plants of Hadauti Plateau of Rajasthan and their Conservation Strategy

Krishnendra Singh Nama*

Abstract

Demand for the pharmaceutical products of Ayurveda is increasing day by day in all over the World, because of the fact that the allopathic drugs have a side effect. Another benefit is low cost and easy availability of herbal therapy. Indian system of medicine has traditionally been used in several neurological disorders. Regular field survey and interviews of local healers were conducted to identify and document the plants which are used for the treatment of mental and neural disorders. The aim of the present study is to understand the knowledge of plants and their taxonomy which used for therapeutic uses. In the present communication Centella asiatica (L.) Urban (Apiaceae), Convolvulus microphyllus L. (Convolvulaceae), and Celastrus paniculatus, Withania somnifera (L.) Dunal (Solanaceae) were used for further use. For each species, vernacular name, part(s) used, medicinal use, method of preparation and applications of the herbal remedies are provided.

Survey study concluded that there is an array of plants used locally to treat mental illness and it is recommended that such surveys are important for documenting our indigenous knowledge. It also focuses on practices related to conservation and sustainable utilization of medicinal plants.

Key Words- Pharmaceutical products, Neural disorders, Mental illness, Herbal therapy

Associate Professor, Department of Botany, M.B.P.G. College, Kota, University Of Kota, Rajasthan, India

Introduction

Herbal remedies are the oldest forms of health care to mankind on the earth. The knowledge of medicinal plants has been used from thousands of years based on different medicinal systems like Ayurveda, Unani and Siddha. In all over the world traditional medicines especially folk or ethno medicines are receiving heightened interest. These age old health care systems are found in close interaction with the nature. Informations regarding traditional herbal medicines had always played a vital role in the discovery of chemotherapeutic agents from plants. In India, it is reported that around 2500 plant species are used by traditional healers [1].

Documentation of this indigenous knowledge is important for the conservation and utilization of biological resources. In the survey, an attempt was made to explore some of useful information on medicinal plants growing in wild and their medicaments in local household remedies by villagers. It is known that western medicines are basically produced from the plants as they have ingredients for drugs. Secondly, the aim of the investigation is to record lesser known/new medicinal uses of plants from the local people/villagers and to know the laws and ways of nature for making optimum sustainable use of plant resources. The protection of large number of medicinal plants in different parts of the India are well documented [2, 3, 4, 5]. Many of the threats to medicinal plant species are similar to those causing endangerment to plant diversity generally. Generally the most serious threats are habitat loss, habitat degradation and over harvesting. But the conservational aspect about the medicinal plants is very rare. Therefore, an attempt has been made to document the knowledge of herbal medicinal plants in the treatment of neural disorders.

For several neurological disorders, modern medicine offers symptomatic treatment that is often expensive and associated with side effects. Indian system of medicine has traditionally been used in several neurological conditions. The accessibility, cost effectiveness and lower incidence of side effects of plant products offer considerable advantages. A survey study was conducted during 2010-2013, concluded that there are some medicinal plants which useful in the treatment of neural disorders. The present paper is an effort undertaken for documentation of this traditional knowledge for future application and scientific investigation of plants in the treatment of neural disorders.

Methodology

Map-1: Satellite Map of Mukundara Hills National Park

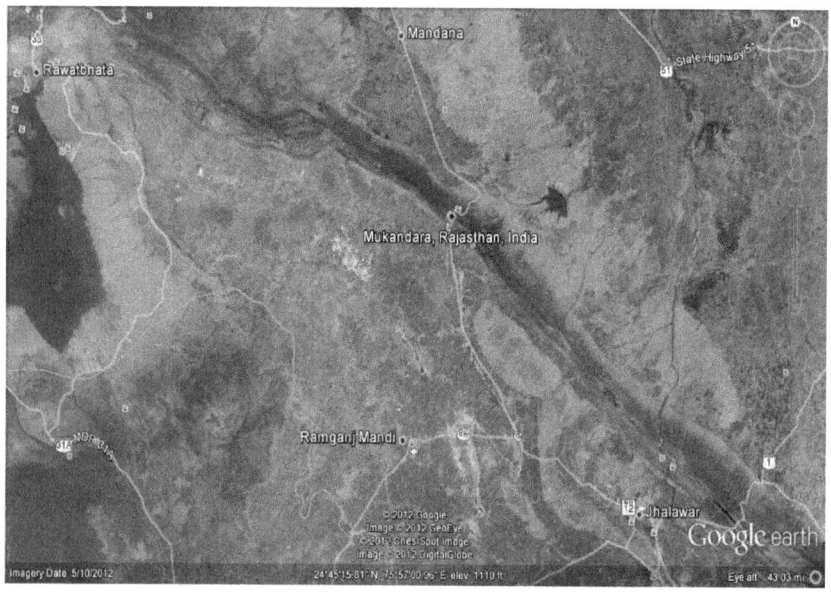

Mukundara Hills Nation Park (Map-1) belongs to the tropical region having a normal annual precipitation of 885.6 mm and with an average 30°C temperature. The soil is of very fertile due to perennial River Chambal. Present study was conducted in throughout the forest during a three year session of 2010-2013 in all three seasons of the year viz. summer, monsoon and winter. During the field survey, ethnomedicinal plants were collected from in and around the forest areas of Mukundara Hills National Park. These plants were preserved as herbarium specimens. Local inhabitants were interviewed about medicinal uses of plants.

Observation-
After careful screening and interviews with the villagers 4 species were selected which are intensively used in the treatment of neural

disorders. These plants are enumerated below with relevant necessary information.

Celastrus paniculatus Wild.
Local Name   Malkangani, Jyotismati
Family   Celastraceae

Uses- For the extraction of oil seeds are placed in a pot of boiling water or goat's milk for over a period of several hours. After some time essential oils rise to the surface, then seeds are strained out, remaining mixture is allowed to settle, finally oil is siphoned out into another container. Oil is stomachoc, tonic, good for cough and asthma; used in leprosy, cures headache and leucoderma. Oil has an efficient therapeutic effect on the central nervous system. Seeds used externally on foul, indolent ulcers and scabies; useful both as an external and internal remedy in rheumatism, gout, paralysis and leprosy [6]. In modern medicinal system Medicated oil extracted from the seeds of the plant is used for topical application as a rubifacient and stimulant. Consumption of half a teaspoon of the oil daily or its application on the head acts as a brain stimulant to improve memory [7].

Status and Distribution in the study area- It is the threatened medicinal plant of the study area and due to its medicinal properties it is going to be extinct in nearby future. It is distributed in localized places of Kolipura range of Mukundara Hills National Park.

Centella asiatica (L.) Urban
Local Name   Brahmi
Family   Apiaceae

Uses: It was described to possess effects on Central Nervous System such as stimulatory-nervine tonic, rejuvenant, sedative, tranquilizer and intelligence promoting agent [8].

Status and Distribution in the study area- It is widely distributed in the study area but decreasing due to overexploitation for medicinal purposes. Found near road side areas of Rawatbhata road.

Convolvulus arvensis L.
Local Name
Family   Convolvulaceae

Uses: The decoction of leaves is used for improvement of mental power and intelligence.
Status and Distribution in the study area- Common on the rocky habitats of Gaipernath Mahadeo.

Withania somnifera (L.) Dunal
Local Name   Ashwagandha
Family   Solanaceae

Uses: Ashwagandha is effective for insomnia but does not act as a sedative. Its rejuvenative and nervine properties produce energy which in turn help the body to settle and sleep. Thus it helps the body to address a stress related condition rather than masking it with sedatives. A herb that rejuvenates the nervous system, erases insomnia and eases stress [9]. Except this root decoction is mixed with milk and given orally to cure sterility in men. Decoction of powdered root is given to ladies in leucorrhoea and frequent miscarriage. Root paste mixed with cow urine is used in skin diseases.

Status and Distribution in the study area- It is widely distributed plant in all over the study area.

Result and Discussion

The present study provides information about the plant species which are mostly used in the treatment of neural disorders since a long time. Proper scientific evaluation of these plants might lead to the discovery of some fruitful information regarding their therapeutical properties. Herbal and ethnomedicinal uses of plants has been reported from a long time but most of these plants do not certified their efficacy. The reported plants were used for various ailments but they need to be pharmacologically screened, chemically analysed and to be tested for a various bioactive compounds. The survey indicates that the flora of Mukundara Hills National Park is rich in medicinal plants and it covers a wide spectrum of human ailments. The area is very important area of plant health in Rajasthan.

References

[1]. Pei, S.J. Ethnobotanical approaches of traditional medicine studies: some experiences from Asia. Pharmaceutical Biology 2001, 39: 74-79

[2]. Vartak, V.D. Kumbhojkar, M.S. and Nipuge, D.S. Sacred groves in tribal areas of Western Ghats: treasure trove of medicinal plants, Bull Medico-Ethno-Bot Res, 1987, 8, 77-78.

[3]. Bhakat, R.K. and Pandit, P.K. An inventory of medicinal plants of some sacred groves of Purulia district, West Bengal Indian For, 2004, 130, 37-43.

[4]. Bhandary, M.J. and Chandrasekhar, K.R. Sacred groves of Dakhina Kanada and Udupi districts of Karnataka, Curr Sci, 2003, 85, 1655-1656.

[5]. Pandit, P.K. and Bhakat, R.K. Conservation of biodiversity and ethnic culture through sacred groves in Midnapore district, West Bengal, India, Indian For, 2007, 133, 323-344.

[6]. Prajapati, H.A., Patel, D.H., Mehta, S.R., Subramanian, R.B. Direct in vitro regeneration of Curculigo orchioides Gaertn., an endangered anticarcinogenic herb. Curr. Sci., 2003. 84: 747-749.

[7]. Nadkarni, A.K. Indian Materia Medica, Popular Prakashan Pvt. Ltd., Bombay, Vol. 1: 1954; 237- 242.

[8]. Veerendra Kumar MH, Gupta YK. Effect of different extracts of Centella asiatica on cognition and markers of oxidative stress in rats. J Ethnopharmacol. 2002;79:253–60.

[9]. Umadevi U. And Kamalam M. Pharmacognostical, phytochemical and heavy etal studies on an ethno medicinal plant- Corallocarpus epigaeus (rottl. & wild.) Clarke. IJPPR; 4(3); 2012; 117-121.

Chapter-III
Conservation and Documentation of Herbal remedies for Neural disorders found in Mukundara Hills National Park, Rajasthan

Kiran Choudhary*

Abstract

The Hadauti region (26° 13' 00"N; 76° 38' 00"E) includes Baran, Bundi, Jhalawar and Kota districts of Rajasthan having area of 24,156.6 Km². This plateau is enriched with floral and faunal diversity. Mukundara Hills National Park and five Sanctuaries viz. Bhainsroadgarh, Darrah, Jawahar Sagar, Ramgarh and Shergarh are wildlife reserves of the area.

Hadauti region can be considered as the repository of valuable and uncommon medicinal plants which are also described in Ayurveda, Siddha and Unani medicinal systems. Intensive field survey on and around the plateau over last 5 years have recorded about 700 wild plant species and nearly 50% of them are used for medicinal purposes. Present study deals with a detailed research thrust of nine endangered but medicinally important angiospermic plants viz. Brahmi (Centella asiatica), Daruhaldi (Berberis asiatica Roxb.), Gudmar (Gymnema sylvestre R. Br.), Guggul (Commiphora wightii (A.) Bhandari), Kalihari (Gloriosa superba L.), Kapilak (Mollutus phillipiensis), Musali (Chlorophytum tuberosum Baker), Akarkara (Anacyclus pyrethrum DC.), and Pakhar (Ficus virens Ait.). Due to some vituperative activities like habitat loss, denudation, and overexploitation of the Medicinal and Aromatic plants (MAP's) diversity of this region is on high stress or may be extinct in long run. The reported plant species have been also declared threatened by the National Medicinal Plant Board, and IUCN. Therefore, some conservation practices should be done to preserve our ancient system of medicine.

Keywords- Hadauti plateau, Threatened plant species, Habitat loss, deforestation, overexploitation.

Ph.D. Scholar, Govt. P.G. College, Kota, Rajasthan, India

Introduction

Rare and threatened plants are an important issue in front of scientific and research community. In India several medicinal plants and their conservation strategies have also been considered [1]. 622 vascular plant species has reported of Indian flora in the Red Data Book till 1990 [2]; this number rose double [3] till 2003, and it is increasing day by day [4]. In India, the rare and threatened species constitute 7.7% of known vascular plant species [3]. Globally, 13.8% of vascular plant species are rare end threatened [3]. Once a species becomes extinct, the particular genetic resource is lost forever. Several conservation measures both in situ and ex situ, has been taken [5/8]. But, plant species are disappearing due to several other reasons [2] and the red list becoming longer. In the present context, the biggest challenge is to conserve plant biodiversity which is threatened by various anthropogenic factors like burgeoning population, over-exploitation to meet the growing demands of people for medicines etc. Systematic vegetation survey undertaken in the Hadauti plateau during 2010-2013 has revealed the list of plants which are nearly threatened in the area. The magnitude of biodiversity loss is so large and so strong that immediate and aromatic plant has to take into consideration the survival of the species on one hand and sustain supply of raw material on the other, to cater to the needs of billions of people throughout the globe.

The present paper is an effort undertaken for documentation of rare and threatened medicinal plants of the study area. This study suggests a few conservation strategies which may be adopted to save the species from extinction risk.

Study Area

Hadauti region (26° 13' 00"N; 76° 38' 00"E) includes Baran, Bundi, Jhalawar and Kota districts of Rajasthan having area of 24,156.6 Km². The most striking geological feature of this region is the Aravalli and Vindhyan ranges. Among them Aravalli is the oldest mountain range in the world and Vindhyachal is in the series of new mountains. This type of geographical position provides variability in climate, edaphic and topographical conditions causes diversity of vegetation in this plateau. This region includes Mukundara Hills National Park and five Sanctuaries viz. Bhainsroadgarh, Darrah, Jawahar Sagar, Ramgarh and Shergarh as wildlife reserves of the area.

The diversity of habitats in this region is reflected in the total number of plant species (c. 700 species) and in the large number of threatened plant species recorded. Majority of the plant species are used for the traditional medicinal system. It has been estimated that about 64% of the total global population depends on the traditional medicine [6]. In India about 85% of the rural population depends on wild plants for their health care [7].

Methodology

Present study was conducted above mentioned study area during a session of five years (2009-2013) in all three seasons of the year viz. summer, monsoon and winter. Extensive field survey was conducted in adjoining forest areas including wild and rural regions to collect the traditional medicinal knowledge and documentation of plant species which are critically threatened, during the survey period. Traditional personals were included as guide and informer for the identification of medicinal plants in their own way. Essential articles like blotting paper, field note book, polythene bags, tags and pencil etc. were used for systemic collection of specimens during regular field survey. These plant samples were collected from their natural habitats, wastelands, and other relevant localities meanwhile the field visits for herbarium purpose. Identification of collected plants was done mostly by the help of relavennt literature [8, 9, 10] and through proper concerning of professional plant taxonomists.

Presentation of these plants were categorised as Endangered and Extinct from Wild (EW en) and critically endangered (CR en) [11]. Major threats to the biodiversity and their probable natural solutions were also studied.

Observation and Result

It is revealed that Hadauti Plateau serves as a biodiversity rich hot spot in special reference to floristic approach. A total of more than 700 Angiosperm belonging to 125 families containing one Gymnosperm species, are recorded across the study sites. Among which 110 trees, 167 shrubs, and 318 herbs and 117 are grass species. The major thrust of the present investigation is Rare and Endangered medicinal plants.

Endangered Medicinal Plants
General information regarding to above categorised plant species of the area with their specific taxonomy, flowering and fruiting period, distribution, medicinal uses and Status is follows:

Centella asiatica (L.) Urban (Apiaceae)
Common Name- Brahmi Buti

Taxonomy- Creeping herb. Leaves broadly suborbicular to reniform, glabrous. Flowers in axillary, fasciculate umbels, pink to red. Fruits ovoid, reticulately wrinkled, primary and secondary ridges distinct.

Fl. & Fr: Almost throughout the year.

Distbution - Not common, found in moist habitats. Keshav Rai Patan and Near Kadap ki Khal of Range Kolipura.
Uses- Used to promote memory power and also to reduce blood pressure. It is mildly antibacterial, antiviral, anti-inflammatory, antiulcerogenic, anxiolytic, nervine and vulnerary, and can act as a a cerebral tonic, a circulatory stimulant, and adiuretic, useful in the treatment of anxiety.

Status in the Study area- Threatened; Least concerned (LC) [12]

Berberis asiatica (Berbidaceae)
Common Name- Daruhaldi

Taxonomy- It is an evergreen Shrub growing to 3.5 m (11ft 6in) at a medium   rate.
It is in leaf in January It is in flower in May. The flowers are hermaphrodite (have both male and female organs) and are pollinated by Insects, self. The plant is self-fertile.

Fl. & Fr: May
Distbution- Extinct from the area.
Uses- Root and bark is used in ophthalmic problems.

Status in the study area- Extinct in Wild (EW); Included in the list of NMPB.

Gymnema sylvestre R. Br. (Asclepiadaceae)
Common Name- Gudmar
Taxonomy- Much branched, twinning shrub. Leaves 3.5-5.5 × 2.5-3.5 cm, ovate, elliptic, acutr, rounded at base, sub-coriaceous. Flowers minute, spirally arranged in lateral pedunculate or nearly sessile cyme, greenish-yellow. Corolla-lobes imbricate. Ridges of corona protruding beyond the mouth of corolla. Follicles usually solitary, 6-8 × 0.8 cm, straight or slightly curved, terete, lanceolate, tapering, glabrous. Seeds c. 1.2 × 0.5 cm, narrowly ovoid-oblong, glabrous, brown.

Fl. & Fr. : April- January

Distbution- Not Common in the deciduous forest. Kolipura Range of Mukundar hills National Park.
Uses- The leaves have been used to treat stomach ailments, constipation, and liver disease. Used to treat diabetes.
Status in the study area- Included in the list of NMPB.

Commiphora wightii (Burseraceae)
Common Name- Guggal

Taxonomy- It is a shrub or small tree, reaching a maximum height of 4 m, with thin papery bark. The branches are thorny. The leaves are simple or trifoliate, the leaflets ovate, 1–5 cm long, 0.5–2.5 cm broad, irregularly toothed. It is gynodioecious, with some plants bearing bisexual and male flowers, and others with female flowers. The individual flowers are red to pink, with four small petals.

Distbution- Not find in wild.
Uses- Gum resin is used in snake bite and scorpion sting. Resin is used in joint care and immune care, increases white blood count. Also used to treat common cold.
Status in the study area- Extinct in Wild (EW); Included in the list of NMPB.

Gloriosa suprba L. (Liliaceae)
Common Name: Kilkari, Kalihari, Lalukheri

Taxonomy- Perennial herb, 1.5-4.0 m high. Leaves sessile, 5.0-12.5 × 1.5-3.0 cm, alternate, opposite, ovate-lanceolate, acuminate, ending in a tendril. Pedicels 5-8 cm long, deflexed at the tip; Flowers axillary, solitary, yellow, tinged with red in upper half, at length completely scarlet. Stamens spreading; anthers dorsifixed. Capsules 2-3 cm long, oblong, septicidal. Seeds many, subglobose.
Fl. & Fr.: August – November.

Distbution- Rare; Found Near Bor Koi in Mukundara NP of Kota District.

Uses- The roots and leaves used in snakebite. Leaves given to cattle as antiworm treatment. Deadly toxic to human beings, used as server ulcer in an optimum dose and cure cancer.

Status in the study area- Near to be extinct; Vulnerable [12]; Included in the list of NMPB.

Mallotus philippensis (Lam.) Muell-Arg (Euphorbeaceae)
Common Name: Senduria, Kanku, Rohan

Taxonomy- Small, much-branched, dioecious, evergreen tree, with thin, dark-grey bark. Leaves 4-25 × 2.5-12.5 cm, alternate, variable in size and shape, ovate-lanceolate, acuminate, slightly-toothed or entire, glandular beneath. Flowers small; male nearly sessile, clustered in terminal erect terminal spikes; female solitary in short spikes. Capsules, 3-lobed, 3-valved. Seeds globose, smooth, black.

Fl. & Fr.: December – March.
Distbution- Naharsingh Mata, Kota Dam of Kota District.
Uses- leaves are bitter, cooling and appetizer. Fruit is heating, purgative, anthelmintic, vulnerary, detergent, maturant, carminative, alexiteric and useful in treatment of bronchitis, abdominal diseases, spleen enlargement etc.
Status in the study area- Critically endangered (CE)

Chlorophytum tuberosum (Roxb.) Baker
Common Name: Dholi Musli, Safed Musli
Taxonomy- Annual herbs, with small root-stock and many cylindric root-fibers ending in ellipsoid tubers. Leaves 20-35 × 2-3 cm, linear-lanceolate, acute, undulate, margined. Scape solitary, simple or branched, with closed, scattered flowers forming dense racemes. Flowers white. Capsules oblong-subglobose, 3-celled; the cells 4 to 6-seeded. Seeds irregularly orbicular, usually compressed, pitted, black.

Fl. & Fr.: August-October
Distbution- Rare in dry deciduous forests; Jamara R.F.
Uses- The drug is employed in bronchitis, opthalmic conditions, vomiting, dyspepsia, lumbago, pain in the joints and in the diseases of nerves. It is considered to have carminative, tonic, aphrodisiac and anti-pyretic properties.
Status in the study area- Threatened

Swertia chirata Buch. Ham.
Common Name- Chirayta

Taxonomy- The plant is an erect annual. The stems are robust, branching, cylindrical below and 4-angled upwards, containing a large pith; the leaves are broadly lanceolate, 5-nerved and sub-sessile; the flowers occur in large panicles, are lurid greenish yellow, tinged with purple; the capsules are egg-shaped, many-sided, sharp-pointed; the seeds are smooth and many- angled. The drug (chiretta) is obtained from the dried plant.

Ethnomedicinal Uses- An astringent stimulantprepared with the plant is an outstanding medication for weak stomach, particularly when it results in indigestion, bloating and nausea. In addition, this bitter tonic is also said to be effectivein protecting the liver. Chirayata is a valuable bitter tonic. It is laxative and an appetizer. It also corrects the disordered process of nutrition and restores the normal function of the system. It is an effective herb for reducing fevers. It isespecially beneficial in the treatment of malarial fevers. It is also effective in hysteria and convulsions. It also show hypoglycemic activity.
Status in the study area- Highly threatened.

Ficus virens Ait. var. virens (Moraceae)
Common Name: Pilkhan/ Pakhal
Taxonomy- Medium sized, deciduous tree, with grey bark. Leaves 5-12 × 2.0-4.5 cm, ovate-lanceolate, glabrous, acute at apex, rounded at base. Receptacles in axillary pairs, globular, glabrous, creamy white. Male flowers sessile, with single stamen; gall and female flowers with 3-4, linear-lanceolate lobes. Achenes smooth.
Fl. & Fr : October – June.

Distbution – Common in wastelands, Kapildhara of Kota District.
Uses- Healing ulcers, skin diseases, cooling, and highly efficacious in threatened abortions, gonorrhea, menorrhagia, leucorrhea, urinary diseases etc.
Status in the study area- Least Concern (IUCN)

Threats to Medicinal Plant Biodiversity
The precious wealth of phyto-biodiversity in the current study area is under various kinds of threat. Several biotic and abiotic pressures are causative factors to make these plants endangered. They include:

Over Exploitation

Over harvesting for commercial uses reduces stocks of wild medicinal plant material. Many pharmaceutical industries (Ayurvedic, Homeopathic, Unani) are over exploiting the medicinal herbs and little efforts have been made to domesticate and bring them under cultivation.

Unscientific Exploitation

Forests are the treasure home for the plants and they are extracted without any scientific knowledge. Hence re-growth and realistic substitution are hampered and this is the major cause of threatens in the wild. Commiphora wightii is an example of such threat [11].

Habitat destruction

Alike animal's plants also prefer their own specific habitat to grow, but due to human activities like illegal mining, uncontrolled grazing though a negative pressure of habitat loss of these plant species.

Environmental Degradation

Interactions between human and environment involve exploitation of natural resources and causing environmental destruction. Natural calamities like soil erosion, intensive cultivation, habitat loss, uncontrolled and unscientific grazing has also led to extinction of some species [13, 14].

Increasing Human Population

Alarmingly increasing human population pressure has resulted in deforestation and over exploitation of natural resources which resulted into the loss of biodiversity.

Genetically Modified Crops

Though gene transfer technology and advance molecular biology has opened a new dimension in global food security but it adverselyaffecting the phytodiversity and sustainable development.

Conservation Strategies

Medicinal plants are renewable natural resources. Therefore, they can be conserved through sustainable utilization which includes both In-situ and Ex-situ conservation. In-situ conservation or on the site conservation is the best and cost effective way of protecting the biological and genetic diversity in its natural habitat. The above said plant species can be protected by adopting following strategies:

Controlled Exploitation of Naturally occurring Medicinal Plants

The persons who exploit the plants for their requirements should know the type of plant form and the part which is used for the preparation of the medicine. It plays a central role in sustainability of wild harvest.

Adopting Extension and Educational Programmes

There should be educational programmes in tribal areas to generate awareness among the local people using audio-visual aids so that they can understand the value of this natural treasure.

Sacred grooves

Sacred grooves are the places of spirituality where conservation activities through local communities help in the management of the biodiversity.

Conclusion

The above said medicinal plants of the present study area are subjected to be lost in the near future. Some are prone to cattle grazing and trampling in addition to large scale collection by local medicinal persons. Over exploitation and habitat destruction leads to ecosystem imbalance and extinction of valuable medicinal species. Lack of systematic collection has resulted in pushing many of the plants into the list of vulnerable, endangered and threatened species. Therefore medicinal plants present a paradox as far as conservation and sustainable use strategies are concerned. Ethnomedicinally important plant group is a heterogeneous assemblage of various plant species with their different characteristics like habit, habitat, morphology, and dynamics of useful phytochemicals. By avoiding destructive harvesting; without affecting the reproduction mode, can ensure survival of threatened medicinal plant species. Last but not least capacity building through on-site training programmes, live demonstrations and interactions between stakeholders and scientists should be facilitated. Government aid alone will not help in this case. Stakeholder and private sector participation is vital in such cases.

References

[1] Jain, S. K. and Rao, R. R. (eds), An Assessment of Threatened Plants of India, Botanical Survey of India, Howrah, 1983, pp. 1–334.

[2] Nayar, M. P. and Sastry, A. R. K. (eds), Red Data Book of Indian Plants, Botanical Survey of India, Calcutta, 1987, vol. 1, pp. 1–371; 1988, vol. 2, pp. 1–273; 1990, vol. 3, pp. 1–279.

[3] Rao, C. K., Geetha, B. L. and Suresh, G., Red List of Threatened Vascular Plant Species in India, ENVIS, Botanical Survey of India, Howrah, 2003, pp. ix–144.

[4] Sanjappa, M., Paul, T. K. and Lakshminarasimhan, P., In Biological Diversity – Origin, Evolution and Conservation (eds Sharma, A. K., Ray, D. and Ghosh, S. N.), West Bengal Biodiversity Board, Kolkata, Viva Books, New Delhi, 2012, pp. 243–251.

[5] Singh, N. P. and Singh, K. P. (eds), Floristic Diversity and Conservation Strategies in India, Botanical Survey of India, Kolkata, 2002, vol. 5, pp. 2341–3090.

[6] Farnworth, N. Ethnopharmacology and drug development. Pp. 42-51. In: Chadwick, D.J. and J. Marsh (Eds.). Bioactive compounds from plants. Cifa foundation symposium, 185, 1994. Wiley, Chichectar.

[7] Jain, S.K. Ethnopharmacology and Drug Development, IN: Ethnobotany and Search for New Drugs, edicted by Chadwick DJ & March U. (Ciba Foundation Symposium 183, Wiley Chichester), 1994.

[8] Singh, V.; Parmar, P.J. and Pandey, R.P., Flora of Rajasthan (Edited by B.V. Shetty & V.Singh). Vol.I, 1987. Botanical Survey of India, Howrah.

[9] Singh, V.; Parmar, P.J. and Pandey, R.P., Flora of Rajasthan (Edited by B.V. Shetty & V.Singh). Vol.II, 1991. Botanical Survey of India, Howrah.

[10] Singh, V.; Parmar, P.J. and Pandey, R.P., Flora of Rajasthan (Edited by B.V. Shetty & V.Singh). Vol.III, 1993. Botanical Survey of India, Howrah.

[11] Jain, S. K. and Sastry, A R. K. Threatened Plants of India. New Delhi: Department of Science "and Technology, 1980.

[12] IUCN Red List Categories and Criteria: Version 3.1. IUCN Species Survival Commission. IUCN, Gland, Switzerland and Cambridge, 2001 UK.

[13] Chaudhary, V., Singh, Karan and Kakralya, B. L. (Eds.). Environmental Protection. Jaipur: Pointer Publishers, 2000, pp. 231-240.

[14] Chaudhary, Y., Singh, Karan; Kumar, A and Bora, K. K. 'Environmentalists, agrihorticuiturists, foresters. industrialists and exporters expectations from phytophysiologists'. In: Production and Developmental Plant Physiology. (Eds.). Bora, K. K., Singh, Karan and Kumar, Arvind. Jaipur: Pointer Publishers, 2001, pp. 5-39.

Chapter-IV

Air Pollution Tolerance Index and Antioxidant Activity of Cassia tora occurring in the Vicinity of Cement Industry

Manpreet Kaur *

Abstract:

Cassia tora is an anthraquinone containing plant, which is widely used in Chinese and ayurvedic medicines. It is very common plant occurring everywhere even in industrial area, road sides in Roorkee, Uttarakhand. In order to study the air pollution tolerance index of Cassia tora, occurring in industrial area of Bhagwanpur, Roorkee, biochemical changes in leaf was assessed. The Antioxidant analysis justify whether the plant is growing in a stressful condition or not, because to relieve from stress it has to scavenge more free radicals to keep them alive. The air pollution tolerance index (APTI)of this plant was 24.87±0.76 Chlorophyll content was 77.76±0.42mg/gm and antioxidant ascorbic acid was found to be high i.e. 12.18±0.89mg/gm. According to our results, ascorbic acid content was high suggesting its role in antioxidant activity. The selected plant Cassia tora was found to be a tolerant species to pollution, its high poly phenol and ascorbic acid content might be playing a major role in imparting antioxidant potential. Likewise, the relative water content is more to manage its survival from stressful environment.

Keywords: Cassia tora, Industrial area, APTI, Antioxidant, tolerant

---

*Research Scholar, Forest Botany Division, Forest Research Institute Deemed University, Dehradun

Introduction

The World Health Organization (WHO) reported that about 80% of the world's population depend mainly on traditional medicine and the traditional treatment involve mainly the use of plant extracts (WHO, 1993). This practice is commonly found in rural areas where synthetic drugs are not available or, where available, are too expensive to purchase. *Cassia tora* is a weed belongs to family Fabaceae, sub-family: Caesalpinioideae, which grows up in warm moist soil throughout the tropical parts of Asian and African countries traditionally reported to have medicinal properties, like laxative, antiperiodic, antihelmintic, ophthalmic, and effective for leprosy, ringworm, flatulence, colic, dyspepsia, constipation, cough, bronchitis, cardiac disorders, etc (Nadkarni, 1985; Chatterjee and Pakrashi, 1992). *C. tora* leaves, seeds and roots are utilized as food ingredients since long (Ingle *et al.*, 2012). Different species of Cassis including *C. tora* are recommended for primary health care in Thailand to treat ringworm and skin diseases (Farnsworth and Bunyaprapatsara, 1992). The roots of *C. tora* are also used in snake bite. The leaves are used during intestinal disorders amongst children. Seeds are externally used in various skin diseases (Sahu, 1984).

Industrialization leads to the increase in pollution in many ways like soil pollution, air pollution by producing waste, dust etc. Emissions of metals from industrial establishments are one of the major sources of environmental pollution. Many heavy metals like Pb and Hg in contaminated soils can be transported by water, wind and other human activities with their resultant health impacts and effects on the environment (Asubiojo et al., 1991). Several reports stated that cement factories have been reported to be a major source of heavy metals emission to the environment showing higher concentrations of heavy metals around cement factories (Isikli et al., 2006; Al-Khashman and Shawabkeh, 2006; Mandal and Voutchkov, 2011). The typical gaseous emissions to air from cement manufacturing plants include nitrogen oxide (NOx), sulphur dioxide (SO_2), carbon oxides (CO & CO_2) and dust (Pregger and Friedrich, 2009; Kampa and Castanas, 2008). The air analysis of cement factory has Pb and Cd (Gbadebo and Bankole, 2007).

Ascorbic acid content (Keller and Schwager, 1977), relative water content (RWC), leaf extract pH (Chaudhary and Rao, 1977), and peroxide activity (Eckert and Huston, 1982) are few parameters that are used in defining sensitivity or resistance of plants towards different air pollutant concentration. Air Pollution Tolerance Index (APTI), an index developed by Singh and Rao (1983) that is used to evaluate the tolerance level of plant species towards air pollution from leaf parameters. Polyphenols, ascorbic acid, are antioxidants, increases under stress, thereby inhibiting the generation of reactive oxygen species and suppressing the generated reactive oxygen species. The plant studied was collected from industrial area, Bhagwanpur which is located in Roorkee and the possibility of vehicular pollution and heavy metal pollution will be more. Hence, an attempt has been taken to study the APTI and antioxidant system which plays an important role in protecting plants against stress. By measuring these parameters we can predict the effectiveness of plant as possibly being suitable in terms of pollution abatement.

Materials and methods

Sample collection
Leaves of *Cassia tora* were collected during April-May 2013 from industrial area, Bhagwanpur, Uttarakhand, India.

Ascorbic acid
Estimation of ascorbic acid was done by method given by Roe and Kuether (1943). The plant extract was prepared in Tris buffer (50 mM, pH-10) under ice cold conditions. The reaction was started with 0.5 ml of extract, 100 mg activated charcoal, 4 ml distilled water and 0.5 ml of 50% TCA. It was mixed well then and filtered with Whatman filter paper No.1 and 0.4 ml of DNPH reagent was added to 1 ml of filterate. The reaction mixture was incubated for 3 hours at 37 °C followed by cooling in ice bath and addition of cold H_2SO_4 (65%). The absorbance was read at 520 nm. The content was calculated by using standard ascorbic acid.

Photosynthetic pigments
The method of Arnon was used to assay the pigments. One gram of shoots was homogenized in 4 ml of 80% acetone under ice cold

conditions. The extracts were centrifuged at 10,000 x g for 15 minutes. The supernatant was used to measure chlorophyll a, b and total chlorophyll spectrophotometrically at the wavelength of 645 and 663 nm.

Leaf extracts pH
0.5 g of leaf sample was crushed and homogenized in 50 ml deionized water, then the mixture was centrifuged and supernatant was collected for detection of pH by a digital pH meter.

Relative water content
The relative water content (RWC) (in percentage) was calculated by using the formula given by Sen and Bhandari (1978):
RWC = fresh weight − dry weight/ turgid weight − dry weight× 10

Evaluation of APTI
Ascorbic acid content, leaves extract pH, total chlorophyll content and relative content of water were taken into account in the form of a mathematical expression to obtain an empirical value, signifying their air pollution tolerance index (APTI) (Singh and Rao, 1983).
$$APTI = A(T + P) + \frac{R}{10}$$
where A is the ascorbic acid content in mg g^{-1} of fresh weight, T the total chlorophyll in mg g^{-1} of fresh weight, P the pH of leaf extract, and R is the relative content of water, in percentage.

Polyphenol Contents:

Polyphenol estimation was done by the method given by Schandari (1970). 0.5 gm of powdered material was boiled with distilled water for 30 minutes. Volume of the supernatant was made up to 100ml by adding distilled water. Folin Denis reagent and sodium carbonate solution were added in known aliquots and absorbance was read at 700 nm after 30 minute.

Proline Estimation:

Proline was extracted from the leaves and estimated by the methods of Bates et al. (1973). Homogenate of the leaf samples were prepared in 3% sulphosalicylic acid. Pink colour was developed by a reaction with glacial acid and ninhydrin. The colour was separated in toluene layer and intensity of the colour was measured at 529 nm. Spectrophotometrically.

Results and Discussion

Study Area

The study area industrial area Bhagwanpur is located in Roorkee, District Haridwar. With the new industrialization policy, new industrial area was came in to existence at Bhagwanpur area of Haridwar district in 2000. Rapid urbanization, industrialization, expansion of the road network and infrastructure has resulted in severe air, soil pollution problem and adverse effects on exposed vegetation. A big cement industry was established which is producing ordinary Portland cement and OPC 33, OPC 43 and OPC 53 grade cement. The cement dust affects the biota as it gets accumulated on leaves and soil nearby the cement factory that are the immediate acceptor of air pollution.

Air pollution tolerance index and antioxidant determination:

Air pollution is common in urban and industrial area, if toxic air pollutants may get absorbed, accumulated or integrated in the plant body, they may injure the plants in various ways (Ishii et al., 2007; Singh et al., 2008).Cement industry caused environmental pollution problems, and the pollutants of the cement industry produced the adverse impact on air water and land. Cement industry is the one of the 17 most pollutant industries listed by central pollution control board (Chaurasia et al., 2013). Cement dust are potentially harmful to the environment. Dust pollution and chronic concentration of gaseous pollutants may affect the biochemical make up and tolerance capacity of plants to the air pollution.

Table Showing Biochemical Changes in Cassia tora

Sr. No.	Parameters Assessed	Observed results (mg/g)
1.	Ascorbic acid	12.18±0.89
2.	Total chlorophyll	7.76±0.42
3.	Carotenoid	5.92±0.11
4.	PolyPhenols	3.9±0.32
5.	Proline	4.8±0.67
6.	pH	6.92±0.33
7.	Relative Water Content	69.9±0.92
8.	Air Pollution Tolerance Index	24.87±0.76

Results observed with *Cassia tora* is depicted in Table 1. The ascorbic acid content of *Cassia tora* was 12.18±0.89 mg/g, pigments like chlorophyll was 7.76±0.42mg/g, relative water content was found to be 69.9±0.92% and the pH was 6.92±0.33. The air pollution tolerance index of the selected plant was 24.87±0.76. So, according to the criterion given by Laxmi *et al.,* 2009, *Cassia tora* was found to be a tolerant species to pollution.

Under stress, in chloroplast, the production of reactive oxygen species (ROS) causes a decrease in content of chlorophyll, Whereas in leaves, the higher ascorbic acid content might be an effective strategy to protect thylakoid membranes from oxidative damage (Tambussi *et al.,* 2000), as ascorbic acid is involved in the defence against ROS produced by the photosynthetic apparatus (Smirnoff, 1996). A high pH improves tolerance against air pollution (Agarwal, 1986). High chlorophyll content (Joshi et al., 1993) and an increased level of ascorbic acid in leaves will increase air pollution tolerance in plants (Chaudhary and Rao, 1977).

Antioxidants behave as a key defence system against free radical mediated toxicity by protecting the damages (Lee et al., 2003). As ascorbic acid can directly scavenge superoxide, hydroxyl radicals and singlet oxygen and reduce H_2O_2 to water via ascorbate peroxidase reaction (Noctor and Foyer, 1998). In our study the ascorbic acid content was found much higher than the control. Scalbert et al. (2005) suggested that polyphenols may protect cell ingredients against oxidative damage and, by that mean they limit the risk of various degenerative diseases associated with oxidative stress. The Polyphenol content of *Cassia tora* observed was 3.9 ± 0.21mg/g that correlates with the results of Shukla *et al.*, 2013 and Carotenoid 5.92 ± 0.35 mg/g. The antioxidant protection requires high amounts of carotenoids, ascorbic acid, alpha tocopherol, glutathione, phenolics and flavonoids (Schoner and Krause, 1990).

There are several stress metabolites, among them; proline is probably the most widespread in plants. Proline accumulation is not only regarded as an indicator of environmental stress but also considered as an important protective role against heavy metal stress (Alia-Saradhi, 1991; Sharma et al., 1998). Here in our study the proline content was found to be high i.e. 4.8 ± 0.67 mg/g.

Conclusion

Biomonitoring of air pollution and its impact on biochemical parameters is extremely relevant in air pollution science. With increased vehicular traffic, industrialization, due to air pollution, there is increasing danger to the biodiversity so determination of air pollution tolerance index is very important. The results of such studies are useful for future planning and may be helpful to -bring out possible control measures. Although, *Cassia tora* is a weed but it is used for medicinal purposes traditionally in different states of India, this study was initiated to have an idea about the air pollution tolerance of the plant. From the observations of the present study, we found that *Cassia tora* is tolerant species to pollution and have high amount of antioxidants.

References:

1. Agarwal SK (1986) A new distributional function of foliar phenol concentration in the evaluation of plants for their air pollution tolerance index. Acta Ecologica 8 (2):29–36

2. Alia-Saradhi PP (1991) Proline accumulation under heavy metal stress. J. Plant Physiol. 138:554–558
3. Al–Khashman OA, Shawabkeh RA (2006) Metals distribution in soils around the cement factory in southern Jordan. Environmental Pollution 140:387–394
4. Arnon DI (1949) Copper enzymes in isolated chloroplasts, polyphenoxidase in Beta vulgaris. Plant Physiol. 24: 1-15.
5. Asubiojo OI, Aina PO, Oluwole AF et al (1991) Effects of cement production on the elemental composition of soils in the neighbourhood of two cement factories. Water Air Soil Pollution 57–58:819–28
6. Bates LS, Waldren RP and Teare, ID (1973) Rapid determination of free proline for water stress studies. Plant and soil 39: 205-208.
7. Chatterjee A and Pakrashi SC (1992) The Treatise on Indian Medicinal Plants, CSIR, New Delhi., Vol. 2. pp. 44-45
8. Chaudhary CS, Rao DN, (1977) A study of some factors in plants controlling their susceptibility to SO_2 pollution. Proceedings of Indian National Science Academy 43: 236–241
9. Chaurasia S, Karwariya A, Gupta AD, (2013) Effect of cement industry pollution on chlorophyll content of some crops at Kodinar, Gujarat, India. Proceedings of the International Academy of Ecology and Environmental Sciences 3(4): 288-295
10. Eckert RT, Huston DV, (1982) Foliar peroxidase and acid phosphate activity response to low level SO2 exposure in eastern while pine clones. Forestry Science 28:661–664
11. Farnsworth NR, and Bunyapraphatsara N, (1992) Thai Medicinal Plants. Recommended for Primary Health Care System. Medicinal Plant Information Center, Faculty of Pharmacy, Mahidol University, Thailand.
12. Gbadebo AM, Bankole OD (2007) Analysis of potentially toxic metals in airborne cement dust around Sagamu, southwestern Nigeria. Applied Science 7: 35-40
13. Ingle AP, Ranaware A, Ladke et al (2012) Cassia Tora: Phytochemical and pharmacological activity. Int. Imperial J. Pharmacognosy Natural Products 2: 14-23
14. Ishii S, Bell JNB, Marshall FM (2007) Phytotoxic risk assessment of ambient air pollution on agricultural crops in Selangor state, Malaysia. Environ. Pollution 150:267-279

15. Isikli B, Demir TA, Akar T et al (2006) Cadmium exposure from the cement dust emissions: A field study in a rural residence. Chemosphere 63:1546–1552

16. Joshi OP, Pawar K, Wagela DK (1993) Air quality monitoring of Indore city with special reference to SO_2 and tree barks pH. Journal of Environmental Biology 14 (2), 157–162

17. Lee MY, Shin HW (2003) Cadmium-induced changes in antioxidant enzymes from the marine alga Nannochloropsis oculata. J. Appl. Phycology 15:13–19

18. Kampa M, Castanas E (2008) Human health effect of air pollution. Environmental Pollution 151: 362-367

19. Keller T, Schwager H, (1977) Air pollution and ascorbic acid. European Journal of Forest Pathology 7:338–350.

20. Lakshmi PS, Sravanti KL, Srinivas N (2008) Air pollution tolerance index of various plant species growing in industrial areas. The Ecoscan 2(2):203-206

21. Mandal, Voutchkov M (2011). Heavy metals in soils around the cement factory in Rockfort, Kingston, Jamaica. International Journal of Geosciences 2: 48-54.

22. Nadkarni AK (1985) Indian Materia Medica. Popular Prakashan, Bombay. Vol. 1. pp. 291-292.

23. Noctor G, Foyer CH, (1998) Ascorbate and glutathione: keeping active oxygen under control. Annu. Rev. Plant Physiology Plant Mol. Biology 49: 249–279

24. Roe JH, Kuether CA (1943) The determination of ascorbic acid in whole blood and urine through the 2,4-dinitrophenylhydrazine derivative of dehydroascorbic acid. J. Biol. Chem 147:399

25. Sahu TR (1984) Less known uses of weeds as medicinal plants. Ancient Science of Life 3(4): 245 – 249

26. Scalbert A, Manach C, Morand C et al (2005) Dietary polyphenols and the prevention of diseases. Crit. Rev. Food Science 45: 287-306. DOI: 10.1080/1040869059096.

27. Schoner S, Krause GH (1990) Protective systems against active oxygen species in spinach: response to cold acclimation in excess light. Planta, 180:383–389

28. Schanderl SH (1970) In: Method in Food Analysis. Academic Press, New York, p.709 Sen DN, Bhandari MC. (1978) Ecological and water relation to two Citrullus spp. In:

29. Althawadi, A.M. (Ed.), Indian Arid Zone. Environmental Physiology and Ecology of Plants 203–228.

30. Sharma SS, Schat H, Vooijs R (1998) In vitro alleviation of heavy metal induced enzyme inhibition by proline. Phytochemistry 46:1531–1535.

31. Shukla SK, Kumar A, Terrence M et al (2013) The probable medicinal usage of Cassia tora: An overview. OnLine J. Biol. Science 13:13-17

32. Singh SK, Rao DN (1983) Evaluation of the plants for their tolerance to air pollution. Proc. national symposium on air pollution control, Indian Institute of Technology, Delhi, pp. 218–224.

33. Singh S, Barman SC, Negi MPS et al (2008) Metals concentration associated with respirable particulate matter (PM10) in industrial area of eastern U.P. India. J. Environ. Biology 29:63-68

34. Smirnoff N (1996) The function and metabolism of ascorbic acid in plants. Annals of Botany 78:661–669

35. Tambussi EA, Bartoli CG, Beltrano J et al (2000) Oxidative damage to thylakoid proteins in water-stressed leaves of wheat (Triticum aestivum). Physiologia Plantarum 108:398–404

36. WHO (1993) Summar 9 WHO guidelines for the assessment of herbal medicines. Herbal Grom 28:13-14.

Chapter- V

Conservation of Biodiversity and Sustainable Use of Medicinal Plants

Anju Batta Sehgal*

Abstract

Biodiversity is variety and differences among living organisms from all sources, including terrestrial, marine, and other aquatic ecosystems and ecological complexes of which they are a part. India is one of the mega biodiversity centers in the world and has two of the world's 18 'biodiversity hotspots' located in the Western Ghats and in the Eastern Himalayas. The forest cover in these areas is very dense and diverse and of pristine beauty, and incredible biodiversity. It is estimated that there exists 5-30 million species of living forms on our earth, of which only 1.5 million have been identified and include 3,00,000 species of plants, 8,00,000 species of insects, 40,000 species of vertebrates and 3,60,000 species of microorganisms. Wide variety in physical features of India and climatic situation have resulted in a diversity of ecological habitats which leads to richness in biodiversity. Climate change has emerged as a most important force of global change, which is resultant of globalization, and mitigation involving global norms and measures. The report of working groups of IPCC assesses the mitigation of climate change. Medicinal and aromatic plants (MAP) have been an important resource for human health care from prehistoric times to present day. According to WHO, majority of the world's human population, especially in developing countries, depends on traditional medicine based on MAP.

* Associate Professor,Department of Botany, Government Post Graduate College Hamirpur, Himachal Pradesh (India)

Introduciton

Oh, the beauty of a forest! The pleasure of walking through it, enjoying the smells of the flowers and the wild; watching the insects flitting about and listening to the birds chirp - how we all love it and wish to return to it again and again. It is this biodiversity that we have to protect and take care of in order to enjoy the joy of it all.

Thus, in essence, biodiversity represents all life. India is one of the mega biodiversity centers in the world and has two of the world's 18 'biodiversity hotspots' located in the Western Ghats and in the Eastern Himalayas[1,] (Myers 1990,). The forest cover in these areas is very dense and diverse and of pristine beauty, and incredible biodiversity. This includes genetic diversity within and between species and of ecosystems. Thus, in essence, biodiversity represents all life. 24% of the global land surface area is occupied by mountains which act as the dwelling place of nearly 12% of world's population and almost 10% of the world's population make use of natural resources for their livelihoods and well being, and many more depends directly or indirectly on them for water, hydroelectricity, timber, biodiversity, minerals, recreation, etc. Himalayan region is highly fragile and susceptible to climate change. The losses are affecting people, their health, besides causing soil erosion, loss of species and change in environmental conditions in the region. The concept of green economy has recently been accepted as one of the significant development models for the future which perks up the well being and social equity, while considerably reducing the environmental risks and ecological scarcities. The idea of green economy has turn out to be a key issue of policy debates. Despite their significant contribution, mountain remained marginalized in the development agenda. Though, the significance of ecosystem services provided by mountains is accepted, methods of estimating the services which need to be recognized and realized, have not yet been developed considerably. Himalayan region is the home of diverse ethnic communities having enormous socio-economic and cultural diversities. The region is gifted with a range of farming systems and rich resource wealth, including biodiversity hotspots & ecosystems sustaining million of people living in the region and also those inhabiting the downstream areas. Mountain ecosystems, offer a range of supporting services, adaptable services, cultural services that sustain and fulfill human life. But the growing demands of ecosystem goods and services are posing threats to the natural resources. The deliberations on the consequences of changing climate and its impacts on ecosystems caught the attention of scientific communities to realize the function and significance of mountains systems. In the recent years, increasing demand and pressure on ecosystems and resources have brought about changes in the mountain system. The importance of biodiversity conservation and management of biological environment in Himalayan region is growing because of projected and perceived effects on terrestrial and aquatic ecosystem.

India is located in south Asia, between latitudes 6° and 38° N and longitude 69° and 97° E. The Indian land mass extending over a total geographical area of about 3029 million hectares, is bounded by Himalayas in the north, the Bay of Bengal in the east, the Arabian sea in the west, and Indian Ocean in the south. The World Health Organization (WHO) estimates that 80 percent of the population of some Asian and African countries presently use herbal medicine for some aspect of primary health care. The paper deals with the principal biological, environmental, social and spiritual effects of climate change on biodiversity. Between 40,000 and 50,000 plant species are known to be used in traditional and modern medicine systems throughout the world. India has sizable no. of endemic flora and fauna. These vary from the humid tropical Western Ghats to the hot deserts of Rajasthan, from the cold deserts of Ladakh and icy mountains of Himalayas to the warm coasts of peninsular India.

The Great Himalayas (27°50' - 27°06' N lat. and 72°30' - 97°25'E) represent the largest mountain chain covering about 5 million km^2 in surface area for which the first Prime minister of independent India, Shri Jawahar Lal Nehru once stated: "Himalayas are not only near to us, but also very dear; for they have always been a part of our history and tradition, our thinking and poetry, our worship and devotion. They are not only physically present in India, dominating the vast Indian plains, but for every Indian they convey a deeper message". Owing to enormous size and elevation, the Himalayas include parts of Trans, North-West, Central and Eastern Himalayas[2] (Rodgers & Panwar, 1990) with as many as 8,000 species of flowering plants (about 50% of the total Indian flora) estimated to occur in this region. From time immemorial, the region has influenced the life and culture of the diverse ethnic communities living all along its length of the mountainous chain (300-8,000m amsl) with vegetation comprising of sub-tropical, temperate, sub-alpine and alpine types.

In the context of climate change, this innate relationship becomes crucial and most important, as the public in general and the poor in particular are dependent on the goods and services supplied by the biodiversity. Hence, it becomes essential to prioritize biodiversity for development and poverty. Round the globe, the poor have been the worst affected and it may accentuate manifold in the context of climate change. This triangular relationship between development, biodiversity and climate change is complex in nature. This is because, development simply means a 'process of desired change' and for any desired change we need raw material which comes directly from the natural setting by more or less affecting biodiversity and the biodiversity of all sorts is struggling for its existence under adverse climatic conditions round the globe.

Loss of Biodiversity

Biosphere constitutes a vital life support system for man. Its existence in a healthy and functional state is essential for the existence of human race. It is the complex collection of innumerable organisms- the bio-diversity- which makes our lives both pleasant and possible. Total number of species on earth is in between 10 million to 80 million[3] (Wilson, 1988), so far only 1.4 million species have been enlisted. Nature has taken more than 600 million years to develop this exceedingly complex spectrum of life forms in biospheres. But we are losing this accumulated heritage at a very fast rate. The very base of our existence is undermined. The onset of biological poverty or reduction in diversity of life forms is bound to have grave consequences for the entire world. Biological diversity is the total variety of life on our planet. The total number of races, varieties or species, i.e., the sum total of various types of microbes, plants and animals present is referred to as biological diversity or simply as bio-diversity. Myers 1988 has identified[4] 12 such localities in tropical regions of world which require urgent conservation attention, these are called as hotspots.

Importance of Biological Diversity

To the human race biosphere is the support system. Each species in this system has its own role and importance. It is a combination of different kinds of living organisms which enables the biosphere to sustain the human race.

Biological Diversity as a Valuable Natural Resource:

Reduction of biological diversity caused by climate change due to globalization, results in disappearance of species of economic value to human race. Large number of useful plants are still wild.

Biological Diversity as a Valuable Genetic Resource:

Old traditional varieties and the wild relatives of domesticated plants and animals constitute a vital genetic resource. No one can anticipate the traits and the genes which shall be needed in future to improve the cultivars of the time as our environment is undergoing rapid changes during the past two to three decades. Reduction in biological diversity shall inflict irreparable damage to future breeding and improvement activities which are necessary to support human society.

Biological Diversity as instrumental of Maintaining a Stable and Healthy Ecosystem:

A system of complex interactions exists between various components of a healthy ecosystem which occur in a state of dynamic equilibrium. Diversity imparts stability to ecosystem.

Biological Diversity as a means of Optimum Utilization and Conservation of Abiotic Resources in an Ecosystem:

Biological diversity serves an ecosystem as an effective instrument which ensure optimum utilization of biotic resources.

Decomposition of organic matter and regeneration of nutrients are very rapid processes due to warm and humid conditions. A wide variety of plants which include large trees, smaller herbs, shrubs, grasses and climbers etc. quickly absorb all the nutrients which are made available to them as the result of mineralisation.

Reduction in Biological Diversity- The Situation Today

Fast rate of extinction of life forms due over exploitation and globalization is causing serious concern. About 300,000 species of flowering plants are known to occur in nature. Large numbers of these species which provide 95% of human food are facing extinction. Nearly 20,000-30,000 species had already become rare and threatened by 1975[5] (Peter Raven 1976).

Medicnal Plants and Their Use

The use of plants as medicines predates written human history. Many of the herbs and spices used by humans to season food also yield useful medicinal compounds. [6] [7] The use of herbs and spices in cuisine developed in part as a response to the threat of food-borne pathogens. Studies show that in tropical climates where pathogens are the most abundant, recipes are the most highly spiced. Further, the spices with the most potent antimicrobial activity tend to be selected.[8] In all cultures vegetables are spiced less than meat, presumably because they are more resistant to spoilage.[9] Angiosperms (flowering plants) were the original source of most plant medicines.[10] Many of the common weeds that populate human settlements, such as nettle, dandelion and chickweed, have medicinal properties.[11][12] A large amount of archaeological evidence exists which indicates that humans were using medicinal plants during the Paleolithic, approximately 60,000 years ago. (Furthermore, other non-human primates are also known to ingest medicinal plants to treat illness)[13][14]

In India, Ayurveda medicine has used many herbs such as turmeric possibly as early as 1900 BC. [15][16] Earliest Sanskrit writings such as the Rig Veda, and Atharva Veda are some of the earliest available documents detailing the medical knowledge that formed the basis of the Ayurveda system.[17] Many other herbs and minerals used in Ayurveda were later described by ancient Indian herbalists such as

Charaka and Sushruta during the 1st millennium BC. The *Sushruta Samhita* attributed to Sushruta in the 6th century BC describes 700 medicinal plants, 64 preparations from mineral sources, and 57 preparations based on animal sources. [18]

Among the 120 active compounds currently isolated from the higher plants and widely used in modern medicine today, 80 percent show a positive correlation between their modern therapeutic use and the traditional use of the plants from which they are derived. [19] More than two thirds of the world's plant species - at least 35,000 of which are estimated to have medicinal value - come from the developing countries. At least 7,000 medical compounds in the modern pharmacopoeia are derived from plants[20] In many medicinal and aromatic plants (MAPs) significant variations of plants characteristics have been ascertained with varying soil traits, and the selective recovery and subsequent release in food of certain elements have been demonstrated. Great attention must be paid to choose soil and cropping strategies, to obtain satisfactory yields of high quality and best-priced products, respecting their safety and nutritional value. [21]

The use of plants as medicines predates written human history. Ethnobotany (the study of traditional human uses of plants) is recognized as an effective way to discover future medicines. In 2001, researchers identified 122 compounds used in modern medicine which were derived from "ethnomedical" plant sources; 80% of these have had an ethnomedical use identical or related to the current use of the active elements of the plant. [19] Many of the pharmaceuticals currently available to physicians have a long history of use as herbal remedies, including aspirin, digitalis, quinine, and opium. The use of herbs to treat disease is almost universal among non-industrialized societies, and is often more affordable than purchasing expensive modern pharmaceuticals. The World Health Organization (WHO) estimates that 80 percent of the population of some Asian and African countries presently use herbal medicine for some aspect of primary health care. Studies in the United States and Europe have shown that their use is less common in clinical settings, but has become increasingly more in recent years as scientific evidence about the effectiveness of herbal medicine has become more widely available. The annual global export value of pharmaceutical plants in 2011 accounted for over US$2.2 billion. [22]

Because "over 50% of prescription drugs are derived from chemicals first identified in plants,"[23] a 2008 report from the Botanic Gardens Conservation International (representing botanic gardens in 120 countries) warned that "cures for things such as cancer and HIV may become 'extinct before they are ever found'." They identified 400 medicinal plants at risk of extinction from over-collection and deforestation, threatening the discovery of future cures for disease. These included Yew trees (the bark is used for the cancer drug paclitaxel); Hoodia (from Namibia, a potential source of weight loss drugs); half of Magnolias (used as Chinese medicine for 5,000 years to fight cancer, dementia and heart disease); and Autumn crocus (for gout). Their report said that "five billion people still rely on traditional plant-based medicine as their primary form of health care."[23] The results of monitoring by TRAFFIC of selected species at high risk show few signs of recovery. [24] As a result the Fairwild Foundation was established in 2008 to promote the sustainable use of wild-collected plant ingredients, with a fair deal for all those involved throughout the supply chain. [25]

References:

1. Myers, N. 1990. The biodiversity challenge: expanded hot-spots analysis. The Environmentalist 10: 242-256.
2. Rodgers, W.A. & Panwar, H.S. 1990. A Biogeographical Classification for Conservation Planning in India. Wildlife Institute of India, Dehradun, India.
3. Edward O.Wilson, editor, Frances M.Peter, associate editor, Biodiversity, National Academy Press, March 1988 ISBN 0-309-03783-2 ; ISBN 0-309-03739-5 (pbk.), online edition
4. Myers N (1988). "Threatened biotas: 'hot spots' in tropical forests". Environmentalist 8 (3): 187–208.
5. Biology of plants. 1976. Raven, Peter H. Biology Library (Falconer) » QK 47.
6. Tapsell LC, Hemphill I, Cobiac L, et al. (August 2006). "Health benefits of herbs and spices: the past, the present, the future". Med. J. Aust. 185 (4 Suppl): S4–24. PMID 17022438.
7. Lai PK, Roy J (June 2004). "Antimicrobial and chemopreventive properties of herbs and spices". Curr. Med. Chem. 11 (11): 1451–60. PMID 15180577.

8. Billing, Jennifer; Sherman, PW (March 1998). "Antimicrobial functions of spices: why some like it hot". Q Rev Biol. 73 (1): 3–49. doi:10.1086/420058. PMID 9586227.

9. Sherman, P; Hash, GA (May 2001). "Why vegetable recipes are not very spicy". Evol

10. Hum Behav. 22 (3): 147–163. doi:10.1016/S1090-5138(00)00068-4. PMID 11384883.

11. "Angiosperms: Division Magnoliophyta: General Features". Encyclopædia Britannica (volume 13, 15th edition). 1993. p. 609.

12. Stepp, John R. & Moerman, Daniel E. (April 2001). "The importance of weeds in ethnopharmacology". Journal of Ethnopharmacology 75 (1): 19–23. doi:10.1016/S0378-8741(00)00385-8. PMID 11282438.

13. Sumner, Judith (2000). The Natural History of Medicinal Plants. Timber Press. p. 16. ISBN 0-88192-483-0.

14. Plant samples gathered from prehistoric burial sites are an example of the evidence supporting the claim that Paleolithic peoples had knowledge of herbal medicine. For instance, a 60 000-year-old Neanderthal burial site, "Shanidar IV", in northern Iraq has yielded large amounts of pollen from 8 plant species, 7 of which are used now as herbal remedies. (see: Solecki, Ralph S. (November 1975). "Shanidar IV, a Neanderthal Flower Burial in Northern Iraq". Science 190 (4217): 880–881. doi :10.1126/science. 190.4217.880.).

15. Aggarwal BB, Sundaram C, Malani N, Ichikawa H (2007). "Curcumin: the Indian solid gold". Adv. Exp. Med. Biol. ADVANCES IN EXPERIMENTAL MEDICINE AND BIOLOGY 595: 1–75. doi:10.1007/978-0-387-46401-5_1. ISBN 978-0-387-46400-8. PMID 17569205.

16. "Turmeric Herb". Tamilnadu.com. 15 December 2012. Sumner, Judith (2000). The Natural History of Medicinal Plants. Timber Press. p. 16. ISBN 0-88192-483-0.

17. Girish Dwivedi, Shridhar Dwivedi (2007). History of Medicine: Sushruta – the Clinician – Teacher par Excellence (PDF). National Informatics Centre. Retrieved 2008-10-08.

18. Fabricant DS, Farnsworth NR (March 2001). "The value of plants used in traditional medicine for drug discovery". Environ. Health Perspect. 109 Suppl 1 (Suppl 1): 69–75. PMC 1240543. PMID 11250806.

19. Interactive European Network for Industrial Crops and their Applications (2000-2005). "Summary Report for the European Union". QLK5-CT-2000-00111. [www.ienica.net/reports/ienicafinalsummaryreport2000-2005.pdf Free full-text].
20. Carrubba, A. and Scalenghe, R. (2012). "Scent of Mare Nostrum — Medicinal and Aromatic Plants (MAPs) in Mediterranean soils". Journal of the Science of Food and Agriculture 92 (6): 1150–1170. doi:10.1002/jsfa.5630.
21. http://www.traffic.org/medicinal-plants/
22. "Medical plants 'face extinction'". BBC News.
23. http://www.traffic.org/medicinal-plants/
24. http://www.traffic.org/medicinal-plants/

Chapter- VI

Achievements of Government of Punjab for Prevention and Control of Dengue through Standard Operating Procedures (SOPs) in Punjab Province, Pakistan

Azhar Hameed, Shazia Pervaiz, Khalida Khan*

Abstract

Dengue is the vector borne disease transmitted by Aedes aegypti and Aedes albopictus. Climate change and environmental degradation is increasing Aedes Aegypti population. Dengue nuisance is the major and challenging health problem in Pakistan especially in the Punjab province. Punjab is dealing dengue since 1982 and severely hit by this major widespread menace in 2010. Punjab's largest city, Lahore is forefront which suffered from the largest number of dengue cases reported more than 14,000 in 2011. Unluckily, the non availability of suitable vaccine of dengue increased the number of deaths and created critical condition for the government to overcome this problem.. To cope up this problem there was only way to prevent vector breeding by following adage "prevention is better than cure." Therefore, Government of Punjab has been set Standard Operating Systems (SOPs) to eradicate vector borne disease. Government of Punjab achieved goal to control dengue by adopting SOPs and 0% deaths reported after it. The aim of this study is to analyze the adopted SOPs by the Government of Punjab to prevent dengue havoc in the country. This study will help researchers and other dengue prone countries to estimate the population of dengue by using time series regression analyses and to find sustainable solution of the dengue prevention by using SOPs of Punjab.
Keywords: Dengue Control, Pakistan, Punjab, Standard Operating Procedures (SOPs), Time, Series Regression.

* Department of Center of Integrated Mountain Research, University of Punjab, Pakistan

Intorduction

Dengue is a worldwide old infectious vector borne fatal disease caused by the vector female mosquito Aedes aegypti or Aedes Albopitus [1] and both vectors of dengue are the species of rural and urban area [2]. Dengue word is derived from the Swahili phrase, "ki denga peopo" and its meaning is "sudden overtaking by a spirit". Dengue Fever is known with different names in different countries for instance break bone fever, boohoo fever, dandy fever, 7 day fever [3]. Dengue is the second largest major cause of mortality after Malaria [4] in tropical and subtropical countries of the world [5].

Dengue Fever (DF)/Dengue Shock Syndrome (DSS) and Dengue Hemorrhagic Fever (DHF) are arboviral diseases comprised by any one of four serotypes DENV-1 to DENV-4 that belong to Family Flaviviridae virus [6]. Estimation of dengue cases depicts that globally 2.5 billion people affected in tropical and subtropical countries by dengue [7]. World Health Organization (WHO) declared that South Asia hit by DF and DHF annually and fifty million dengue cases document every year [8].

According to Weaver [9] the aggressive dengue spreads in warm climate. Precipitation, humidity, temperature are the favorable aiding variables of climate for the growth and survival of Aedes Agepty [10]. The suitable temperature for the growth of dengue vector is 15 to 30°C [11]. Global warming [12] is helping to increase the number of dengue vector but there are some other major additional contributing factors playing a vital role for the dengue breeding. Poor socioeconomic conditions, poor urban areas, inadequate water supply and poor sanitation are the perfect breeding habitats for dengue mosquito [13, 14].

Dengue Perspective in Pakistan

Pakistan is facing an antagonistic outbreak of dengue fever after rainy season since early 90s [15]. Aedes aegypti and Aedes albopictus both are major vectors of dengue in

Pakistan and found in different geographical areas of the country. Southern parts of the country having elevation above 24-50 metres sea level are dominant by Aedes Aegypti and Northern mountainous and sub mountainous parts of the country above 500-600 and 2500 metres sea level are reported significantly dominated by Aedes Albopictus. Central part of the country is dominant by Aedes Aegypti but the reasonably Aedes Alobpitus has found in high density in these areas [16].

Environmental determinants are the root causes of mosquito borne diseases [17]. Similarly in Pakistan vector borne disease is closely associated with climatic conditions, over urbanization, improper sanitation, residing of large number of refugees, and absence of dengue vaccination [8] and these are the main reasons of dengue endemic in Pakistan [18]. Rainy season [19] of Pakistan and especially post monsoon period is optimal for breeding of dengue vectors and became the major epidemiological threat for the country [8].

In 1985, first dengue fever case was reported in Pakistan [20] and in 1994 the first major outbreak of dengue was reported in Karachi [21] and out of 145, 1 patient died [22]. Punjab is the largest endemic province of Pakistan having 56% population. In 2011 devastating outbreak of dengue occurred in Punjab Province of Pakistan. Lahore is the capital city of Punjab that hit severely by dengue. Maximum deaths by Dengue Fever reported from Lahore [23]. To cope up this health problem the Government of Punjab took initiative. After eighteenth amendment in the constitution in the Islamic Republic of Pakistan, health is the primary responsibilities of the provincial governments [24].

This article has been prepared with an objective to analyze the Standard Operating Procedures (SOPs) used by the Government of the Punjab to control the nuisance of dengue in the province. This study is based on the literature review of dengue and SOPs. Time series analysis is also used in this study to evaluate the achievements of the Government of the Punjab by using SOPs. This study help researchers and other dengue affected countries to control dengue.

Material and Methods

Punjab is the 2nd largest province in terms of Land at 205,344 km² of Pakistan with 56% of the total population of the country. Lahore is the capital and the largest city of Punjab. Other important cities of Punjab are Sheikupura, Faisalabad, Multan, Bahawalpur, Sialkot, Gujranwala, Sargodha, Gujrat, Jehlum, and Rawalpindi. Five rivers flow through Punjab from west to east named as Ravi, Sutlej, Chenab, Jhelum and Indus. Punjab is the only provice which touches all the provinces. Punjab is the most fertile region with river valleys.

Punjab province were selected for the study sites. Punjab government and its institutions set strategies the prevention of dengue in Punjab. A Quantitative time series data was collected to establish an estimated second degree parabola.

Table Showing Number of dengue infection reported
annually Years and No. of dengue infections (y)

Years	No.of Infections y	x	x2	x3	x4	xy	x2y
2004	25	0	0	0	0	0	0
2005	500	1	1	1	1	500	500
2006	5400	2	4	8	16	10800	21600
2007	2700	3	9	27	81	8100	24300
2008	1800	4	16	64	256	7200	28800
2009	570	5	25	125	625	2850	14250
2010	5000	6	36	216	1296	30000	180000
2011	20000	7	49	343	2401	140000	980000
	35995	28	140	784	4676	199450	1249450

$$y = a + bx + cx^2$$
$$\sum y = n\,a + b \sum x + c \sum x^2 \;\text{---------------- I}$$
$$\sum xy = a\sum x + b \sum x^2 + c \sum x^3 \;\text{----------- II}$$
$$\sum x^2 y = a\sum x^2 + b \sum x^3 + c \sum x^4 \;\text{------ III}$$

$$35999 = 8a + 28b + 140c \text{ ----------------I}$$
$$587628 = 336\,b + 2352\,c \text{ ----IV}$$
$$199450 = 28a + 140b + 784c \text{ -------------II}$$
$$7061600 = 2352\,b + 21112\,c \text{ ---V}$$
$$1249450 = 140a + 784b + 4676\,c \text{ -------III}$$
$$\Rightarrow c = 634.2952, \quad b = -2691.17, \quad a = 2818.816$$
$$Y = 2818.816 - 2691.17\,x + 634.2952\,x2$$

Results

According to the above time series regression equation, the estimated value of dengue patients in 2015 = 39336 app. A dangerous number of dengue infection were estimated through this analyses. If Govt. of the Punjab would not took immediate and proper action through its suitable SOPs, then there will be the great disaster for the inhabitants of Punjab, Pakistan.

Guidelines/SOPS on Dengue Control

To eradicate dengue infection the Chief Minister (CM) of Punjabe directed to set proper guidelines and SOPs related to the spread of dengue infection. To fight with exceptional Dengue Epidemic of 2011, government of the Punjab used all its resources succeeded in the prevention of dengue disease. Guidelines and SOPs adopted under the guidance local and international experts. All government institutions whether they were linked directly or indirectly in the prevention and control dengue. As discussed above through statistical analysis, Punjab was going into the dangerous level of dengue infection, so a complete and long term plan for the prevention and control of the dengue required. Hence the institution's duties were redefined and developed new system through SOPs in a way to implement through Health Departments and other Allied departments. These SOPs were arranged to set a detailed system for the prevention and control of dengue. Through these SOPs individuals and govt. institutions were clearly defined their roles and responsibilities within a given timelines. It was expected that through the implementation of SOPs, the province of the Punjab would start its success towards elimination of the dengue menace.

Institutional Arrangements

Different committees were established by the Govt. of the Punjab, these are given this figure:

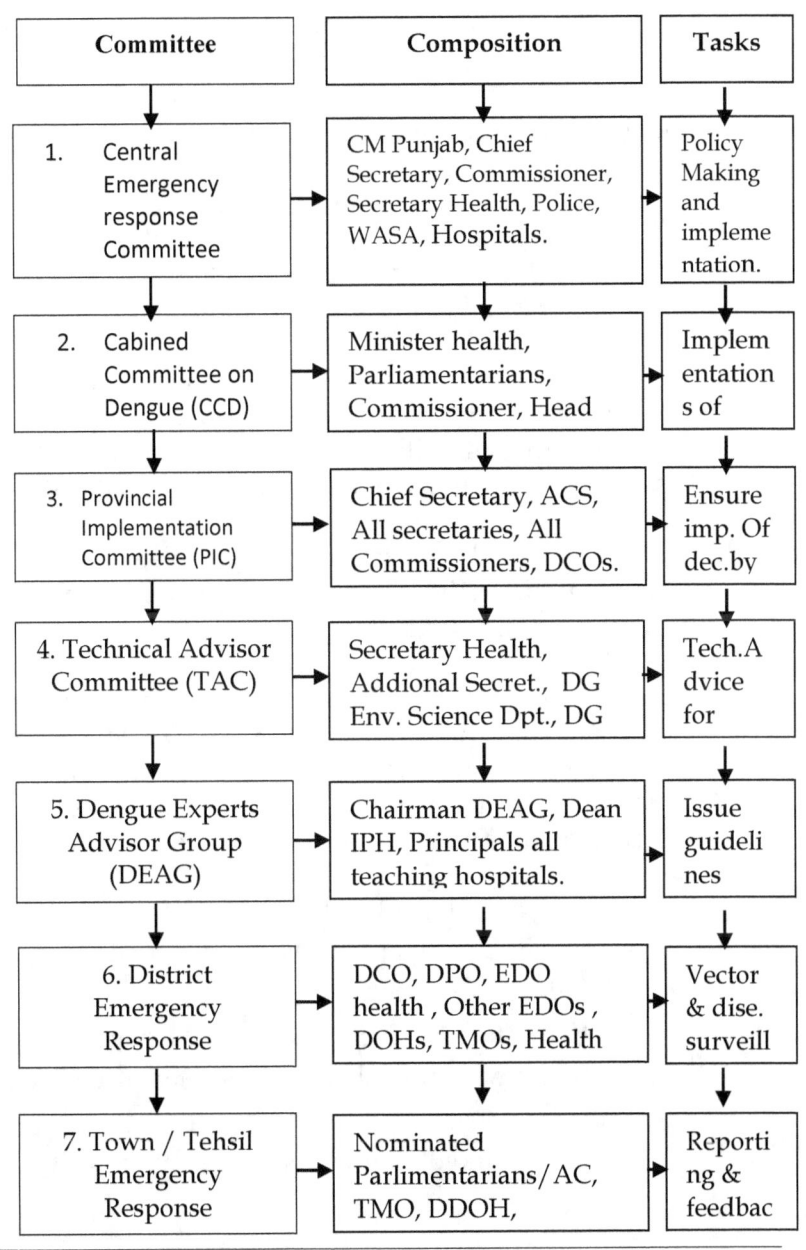

Committee	Composition	Tasks
1. Central Emergency response Committee	CM Punjab, Chief Secretary, Commissioner, Secretary Health, Police, WASA, Hospitals.	Policy Making and impleme ntation.
2. Cabined Committee on Dengue (CCD)	Minister health, Parliamentarians, Commissioner, Head	Implem entation s of
3. Provincial Implementation Committee (PIC)	Chief Secretary, ACS, All secretaries, All Commissioners, DCOs.	Ensure imp. Of dec.by
4. Technical Advisor Committee (TAC)	Secretary Health, Addional Secret., DG Env. Science Dpt., DG	Tech.A dvice for
5. Dengue Experts Advisor Group (DEAG)	Chairman DEAG, Dean IPH, Principals all teaching hospitals.	Issue guideli nes
6. District Emergency Response	DCO, DPO, EDO health , Other EDOs , DOHs, TMOs, Health	Vector & dise. surveill
7. Town / Tehsil Emergency Response	Nominated Parlimentarians/ AC, TMO, DDOH,	Reporti ng & feedbac

Integrated Vector Surveillance

Integrated Vector Surveillance was based on continuous monitoring of the vector population. This monitoring data was directly linked with the daily average temperature both min & max along with rain and humidity % (RH). As temperature of the Punjab vary from 10 C° to 24 C° both are favourable for adult population. Therefore it was directed based on the last two years 2012, 2013 that the IVS should not be delayed beyond 15th Feb of 2014.

Each UC was given a plan to monitor the vector population and vector density. With the help of collected information from each UC, It was strictly directed that negligence will not be tolerated during the high breeding time.

A certification program of IVM introduce vector training which was equipped for all field force which is directly or indirectly linked with chemical application. EDOHs was assigned to get sample of all households in each UC.

Random Sampling technique was planned to use for sampling frame. This technique was used to visit distinct houses over next 10 days.

Each UC had to make three teams including 2 staff members with one female in each team to visit a 75 houses daily. The teams were ensure vector surveillance of each house visited. The data was arranged on a form submitted to the EDOH daily for entry into the database prepared by the PITB.

This activity continue till date:
- The data stored in the database is used to for Breateau Index & Container Index.
- If the larval development got in one container, that house was marked with it's around also checked with red big mark.
- The marked house was on high priority to have continuous checking till the clearance by the team.

- If a UC was on high risk, sweeping activity was started by EDOHs o volunteers.
- Alert Generation Team (AGT) was the responsible authority to generate vector indices mentioned by the Technical Advisory Committee (TAC).
- All teams which were assigned for surveillance and cleanliness of households had to ensure mechanical elimination of breeding. Biological/Chemical treatment was referred only at those places where mechanical elimination was not possible.
- Fogging and IRS was done if the TAC recommended. Fogging & IRS activities was followed as per WHO guidelines & doses was used by the company's recommendations on the containers.
- EDOH office was responsible to maintain records of the consumption of insecticides provided by the field teams.
- Dengue Act was strictly implemented by the authorized government officers.
- Android mobile sets were given to field teams to send online pictures of the visited areas.

Arrangements for the Logistics:
Sentinel Lab: Sentinel lab were established at Lahore.
Entomological Lab: Established mosquito insectary at IPH Lahore Clinical Care Provisions: Established/ maintained Dengue labs, counters and wards by concerned facility authorities.

Annual Procurement
Insecticides:
Only those products were used which were approved by WHO along with doses by DGHS of the Punjab. Procurement was finalized by the end of December.

Private sector had to use of insecticides after testing as per standard by the government.

Spray Equipment Procurement/ Maintenance:

Regular inspection and of all Entomological Lab and inline and stock of spray equipment and Personal protective equipment (PPE) spatially in December by all EDOHs & DGHS for the availability by 10th of February annually.

Health Line Centre: Call Centre were established under PITB with phone line: 080099000)

Capacity Building:

Training need assessment in December of each year.

Continuous updating of modules prepared by IPH, DEAG & DGHS

Create Master Trainers and training of new staff, surveillance teams' media health teams at Provincial level.

Health Education and Social Mobilization:

Health department established public awareness messages by DGHS.

District Government was responsible for awareness campaign through:

Print / electronic media, Cable networks, TV talk shows, Banners, posters, pamphlets, Door to door campaign, Mobilization of school/college teachers & students, health sessions, Mobilization of NGOs.

Dengue days appropriately observed by CERC Committee.

Behaviour Change Communication (BCC):

The DG Health Punjab issue advisories & guidelines for prevention and control of vector borne diseases.

Master trainers arranged for health education through different methods like personal and group discussions, social welfare society meetings and school/college teacher and students volunteers from all districts.

Pre-Monsoon Activities:
June and July are the months which require cleanliness everywhere in the town.

Following activities were undertaken:
- First week of July was critically observed for cleanliness.
- Local government, NGOs and LGCD were assigned to keenly observe the locations of water contamination, constructions sites, door to door, tyres shops, graveyards, junkyards, public parks, hospitals, parking and public places to eliminate dengue breeding.

Operational Research:
Chief Minister of the Punjab established a Research & Development Cell with the help of Institute of Public Health Lahore and the University of Agriculture Faisalabad and assigned to to assess the diverse dynamics of vector and virus for making control strategies.

Legislative Support:
It is necessary to have legislation which ensures prevention of mosquito genic conditions. Provincial Assembly approved an Act and implemented to ensure the preventions of mosquito breeding. TAC had the authority to nominate a committee to formulate/ review this Act for the dengue prevention and proposed improvement in following:
Model civic byelaws: Under this act heavy fine and punishment is imparted, if larva is detected.
Building Construction Regulation Act: Under this act it was ordered to make buildings by not allowing mosquitoes breeding due to water stagnation.
Environmental Health Act: Under this act the proper disposal of junk, old tyres, tins, and other debris.

Health Impact Assessments: Appropriate legislation was formulated for any development projects.
Insecticide regulation laws: An act was formulated to stop the use of inappropriate and non approved insecticides by the WHO.

Housekeeping Activities:

All teams were involved in this activity and the reports were sent to DGHS and CM secretary on regular basis. These activities are:

- Keep the environment neat and clean by removing of room cooler, AC, rain water, extra water in plants pots and garbage.
- Insecticide spray in corners of the rooms.
- Roofs must be neat and clean.
- There should not be leakage of water from drain or pipes.
- Door to door awareness visits.
- Seminars in school, colleges and other government institutions.
- Dispose off unnecessary old records, furniture, papers, e-material etc.
- Daily classes in school / colleges on dengue prevention and control.

Conclusion

Dengue Fever is the deadly threat in Pakistan. In order to prevent and control the dengue epidemics we have to set some SOPs as discussed in this paper. As there is no proper vaccine for the dengue fever so we have to control dengue epidemics by changing our habits through adopting the above discussed SOPs set by the Govt. of the Punjab. In the end but not the least there is only one way to prevent and control of dengue and to save human's precious life that is to change our habits of spending life.

References

[1] N. Sivagnaname, S. Yuvarajan, R.L.J. D. Britto, Urgent need for a permanent dengue surveillance system in India, Current Science, 102(5), 2012, 672-675.

[2] L. A. P. Nguyen, A. C. A. Clements, J. A. L. Jeffery, N. T. Yen, V. S. Nam, G. Vaughan, R. Shinkfield, S. C. Kutcher, M. L. Gatton, B. H. Kay, P. R. Rayan, Abundance and prevelance of aedes aegypti immautres and relationships with household water storage in rural areas in southern Viet Nam, International Health, 3(2), 2011, 115-125.

[3] R. R. Hesse, Molecular evolution and distribution of dengue viruses type 1 and 2 in nature, Virology, 174, 1990, 479-493.

[4] U. Raheel, M. Faheem, M. N. Riaz, N. Kanwal, F. Javed, N.S.S. Zaidi, I.Qadri, Dengue fever in the Indian subcontinent: An overview, J Infect Dev Ctries, 5, 2011, 239-247.

[5] A. Sarkar, D. Taraphdar, S. Chatterjee, Molecular typing of dengue virus circulating in Kolkata, India in 2010, Journal of Tropical Medicine, 2011, 10:1155.

[6] A. Abbas, R. Z. Abbas, J. A. Khan, Z. Iqbal, M. M. Hayat, Z. D. Sindu, M. A. Zia, Integrated strategies for the control and prevention of dengue vectors with particular reference to aedes aegypti, Pakistan, Pakistan Veterinary Journal, 34(1), 2014, 1-10.

[7] D.R.D. Guedes, M.T. Cordiro, M.A.V. Melo-Santos, T. Magalhaes, E. Marques, L. Regis, A.F. Furtado, and C.F.J. Ayres, Patient based dengue virus surveillance in aedes aegypti from Recife, Brazil, J vector Born Dis, 47, 2010, 67-75.

[8] F. Jahan, Dengue fever (DF) in Pakistan, Asia Pacific Family Medicine, 10(1), 2011, 1.

[9] T.Weaver, S. Cooper, N. Vasilakis, Molecular evolution of dengue viruses: contributions of phylogenetics to understanding the history and epidemiology of the preeminent arborial disease, Journal of Molecular Epidemiology and Evolutionary Genetics in Infectious Diseases, 9(4), 2009, 523-540.

[10] P. Aracri, N. Tapper, S. Pfueller, Regional variability in relationship between climate and dengue/DHF in Indonesia, Singaporean Journal of Tropical Geography, 28(3), 2007, 251-272.

[11] H.M. Yang, M.L.G. Macoris, K.C. Galvani, M.T.M. Andrighetti, D.M.V. Wanderley, Assessing the effects of temperature on the population of aedes aegypti, the vector of dengue, Epidemiology and Infection, 137(8), 2009, 1188-1202.

[12] K.L. Gage, T.R. Burkot, R. J. Eisen, E. B. Hayes, Climate and vector borne diseases, American Journal of Preventive Medicine, 35(5), 2008, 436-450.

[13] A. Amin, R. Talib, S. Raza, Extract association rules to minimize the effects of dengue by using a text mining technique, International Journal of Computer Science and Mobile Computing, 3(4), 2014, 394-400.

[14] N.G. Gratz, Critical review of the vector status of aedes albopictus, Medical and Veterinary Entomology, 18(3), 2004, 215-227.

[15] S. Ahmed, W.W. Mohammad, F. Hamid, A. Akther, R. K. Afzal, A. Mahmood, The 2011 dengue haemorrhagic fever outbreak in Lahore- An account of clinical parameters and pattern of haemorrhagic complications, Journal of the College of Physicians and Surgeons Pakistan, 23(7), 2013, 463-467.

[16] Government of Pakistan (GoP), National Guidelines for Dengue Vector(s) Control in Pakistan, The Ministry of National Health Services, Regulations and Coordination, Islamabad, Pakistan, 2013, retrieved in August, 2014 from http://www.dmc.gov.pk/ documents/GDC/ itlePage_ FINAL_Pic.pdf

[17] M. Palaniyandi, The environmental aspects of dengue and chikungunya outbreaks in India: GIS for epidemic control, International Journal of Mosquito Research, 1(2), 2014, 38-44.

[18] M. Sarwar, Dengue fever as a continuing treat in tropical and subtropical regions around the world and strategy for its control and prevention, Research and Reviews: Journal of Pharmacology and Toxicological Studies, 2(2), 2014, 1-6.

[19] A. Almas, O. Parkash, J. Akhter, Clinical factors associated with mortality in dengue infection at a tertiary center, Southeast Asian J Trop Med Public Health, 4(12), 2010, 333- 340.

[20] J.A. Qureshi, N.J. Notta, N. Salahuddin, V. Zaman, J.A. Khan, An epidemic of dengue fever in Karachi; associated clinical manifestations, The Journal of the Pakistan Medical Association, 47(7), 178-181.

[21] B. Jamil, R. Hasan, A. Zafar, K. Bewley, J. Chamerlain, V. Mioulet, M. Rowlands, R. Hewson, Dengue virus serotype 3, Karachi, Pakistan, Emerg InfectDis, 13(1), 2007, 182-183.

[22] S.T. Hakim, S. M. Tayyab, S.U. Qasmi, S.G. Nadeem, An experience with dengue in Pakistan: An expanding problem, Ibnosina J Med BS, 3(1), 2011, 3-8.

[23] E. Khan, R. Hasan, Dengue interaction in Asia; A regional concern, J Postgard Med inst, 26(1), 2011, 1-6.

[24] M. Luqman, T. Sattar, S. Farid, W. A. Khan, Effects of dengue incidence on socio-economic status of patient's family: A comparative analysis of Multan and Lahore City Pakistan, Journal of Economics and Sustainable Development, 4(13), 2013, 28-39.

Chapter- VII

Health Status in Himachal Pradesh: A Geographical Study

Suman, Smita Bhutani, Simrit Kahlon*

Abstract

Health is an important aspect of well being. One needs good health to lead an economically productive life. The health of individuals and communities depends upon various socioeconomic, demographic and environmental factors. The objective of the present study is to analyse the health status in Himachal Pradesh. An attempt has also been made to examine the extent to which environmental factors such as sanitation, access to safe drinking water and have affected the health status in the state. To understand the status of health an analysis of indicators such as infant mortality rate, death rate, birth rate and life expectancy has been employed through various quantitative techniques like composite index, correlation analysis etc.. The study depends entirely on secondary data. The relevant secondary data has been collected from various dependable sources, both official and non-official or private agencies. Although the level of health status in Himachal Pradesh has shown substantial improvement over the years, yet there are marked inter-district variations in health achievements of the state and some of the districts are at a deplorably low level of health.

Key words: Health Status, Health Services, Environmental Factors nd health achievements

* Research Scholar, Professor, Department of Geography, Panjab University, Chandigarh

Introduction

"The health of people is the foundation upon which all their
happiness and all their powers as a state depend"
– Benjamin Disraeli, (1877)

Health, as defined by World Health Organisation (WHO 1948), is a
state of complete physical, mental and social well-being and not
merely the absence of a disease or infirmity to lead a socially and
economically productive life [1]. And, it is vital for ethical,
aesthetic, material and spiritual development of man. Health
therefore becomes one among the most crucial requirements for any
society's development, especially the developing ones. And it is also
an important aspect for human welfare. As a Gujarati proverb says
"the first happiness is health, the second is a full stomach". One
can't enjoy food if one is not healthy (of course, one cannot be
healthy if one doesn't have enough food). The level of health status
in any region is a manifestation of human well- being. Better health
is central to human happiness and well-being. It also makes an
important contribution to economic progress, as healthy populations
live longer, are more productive, and save more [2]. Perception
about physical well being, mental well being and social well being
and so on differs from person to person, from one community to
another, from one geographical region to another, from one time of
point to another, and from one information/technology state to
another state [3].

A statistical association between human resources for health (HRH),
intervention coverage, environmental variables and health outcomes
is of great importance. The relationship between availability of
doctors, nurses and midwives across countries and intervention
coverage (the percentage of deliveries with skilled birth attendance
and the proportion of children fully immunized against measles) was
explored by Chen et al. (2004) and Anand & Barninghausen (2006),
who also examined the relationship with maternal, infant and under-
five mortality[4][5]. Health status and levels of coverage are
positively associated with health worker density (defined as the
number of health workers per 1000 population) [6]. Gupta et.al.
(2011) demonstrated findings from 68 countries that availability of
doctors, nurses and midwives is positively correlated with coverage

of skilled birth attendance [7]. Infant mortality rate and under five child mortality rates are consistently lower among children living in families who accessed drinking water from a safe source as compared to those who accessed drinking water from an unsafe source. Similarly, the infant mortality rate and under five mortality rates were consistently lower among children living in families with access to an improved toilet as compared to those who did not have such a facility. However, an adverse effect of unsafe source of drinking water and unhygienic toilet facilities diminishes after adjustment for demographic and socio-economic factors [8]. Morale et al (2002) also suggested that the health of a population is greatly determined by the social and economic circumstances of that population, as well as its access to health care services [9].

The study described by Mostafa (1973) examined the relationship between socio- economic status and mortality from nine leading causes of death [10]. Mahesh (1980) showed the associations between specific health service and environmental variables and the infant mortality rates of Sri Lanka and examined these both across regions and through time [11]. The world's one sixth population lives in India. The state of the health of the Indians has a significant bearing on the state of the world's health. About 40 per cent of the people cited health as their main concern before other issues such as financial problems, housing or crime .Indian states can be compared with the rest of the developing countries, health performance of some states is no better than worst countries of the world [12]. There are so many plans, health programmes and goals for achieving high health status since independence.

Table Showing State wise Health Status Indicators in India

Sr. No.	States	Crude Birth Rate (2011)*	Crude Death Rate (2011)*	Under Five Mortality Rate (2012)**
1.	India	21.8	7.1	59
2.	Assam	22.8	8.0	83
3.	Bihar	27.7	6.7	64
4.	Gujarat	21.3	6.7	56
5.	Haryana	21.8	6.5	55
6.	Himachal Pradesh	16.5	6.7	49
7.	Jammu& Kashmir	17.8	5.5	48
8.	Kerala	15.2	7.0	15
9.	Punjab	16.2	7.0	43
10.	Rajasthan	26.2	6.7	69
11.	Uttar Pradesh	27.8	8.1	70

Source: *Sample Registration System of India, 2011[13]
        ** Estimates From National demographic and Mortality
Surveys, Published by Lancet Global Health (2013)[14]

Study Area

Himachal Pradesh is a hilly state located in the north- west of the country. There are wide physical variations ranging from low hills to high mountains with lakes and flowing rivers in the state. The state has an area of 55, 673 sq. km, and it accounts for 1.75 percent of India's total geographical area. The state is having 12 districts with a population of 68, 64,602. The density of population is 123 persons per sq.km. Himachal Pradesh with an urban population of only10.03 percent of the total population has 56 cities and towns. The majority (89.9) of the population is in rural habitations varying in size from isolated hamlets to conglomerated settlements. About the half of the area is covered under the tribal belt with a population of just 5.71lakh [15]. Due to peculiar topography the population size of district varies. It varies from a high of 15.10 lakhs in Kangra to a low of 31.5 thousand in Lahaul & Spiti. In spite of that Himachal Pradesh has made significant development on demographic front and stands at 3rd rank followed by Kerala and Punjab in Human

Development Report [16]. Himachal Pradesh also performs well in terms of crude birth rate, crude death rate and under five mortality rate as compared with other states.(Table-1) but there are still large differences in these indicators at district level in Himachal Pradesh. So, through this paper an attempt is made to understand differences in the level of health status at district level in the state.

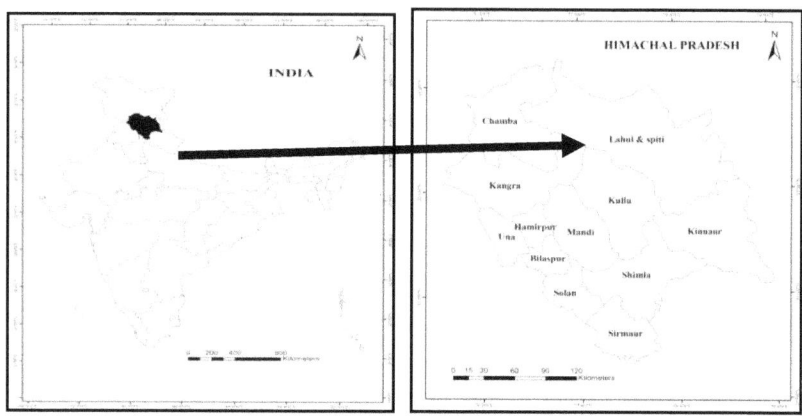

Objectives
To study the patterns of health status in terms of crude birth rate, crude death rate and under five mortality at district level in Himachal Pradesh

> *To examine the effects of environmental variables such as access to safe drinking water and availability of sanitation facilities; and health services variables such as availability of doctors and nurses on health status*

Data Sources and Limitations
Health is difficult to measure. For want of better indicators, the health status of people is generally assessed by measurement of crude birth rate, crude death rate, child mortality, morbidity as well as life expectancy at birth. These indicators of health are determined by numerous factors such as per capita income, nutrition, housing, sanitation, safe drinking water, social infrastructure, health and medical care services provided by government, geographical location, climate, employment status and incidence of poverty [17][18]. These inter-related aspects are so complex that gauging them in absolute terms is very difficult.

For the present study, data for crude birth rate and crude birth rate are derived from District Statistical Abstract of Himachal Pradesh (2011) and data for under five mortality is taken from Lancet Global Health (2013). Data for health services variables such as availability of doctors and nurses has been procured from Directorate of Health Services Shimla (2011). For getting information related to drinking water and sanitation facilities in the state, Census of India (2011) has been widely utilized. Due to unavailability of data at lower level, district has been considered as the study unit for the present work. The major limitation of the study is that data has been derived from various sources. Using the same data source for different indicators to identify the health status is not possible due to the unavailability of complete data with one single source. Different sets of data for health status indicators have been tapped from different sources.

The present study measures health status in terms of crude birth rate, crude death rate, under five mortality rate and effects of environmental variables in terms of access to safe drinking water, availability of sanitation facilities and availability of doctors and nurses at district level in Himachal Pradesh during the period 2010-11.

Methodology
To understand the level of health status of population in Himachal Pradesh, the selected indicators are:
> Crude Birth Rate
> Crude Death Rate
> Under Five Mortality Rate

For calculating health status of Himachal Pradesh, the following methodology is adopted:

Step I: Index value separately of Crude Birth Rate, Crude Death Rate and Under Five Mortality Rate is calculated for all districts of the state.

> Index value of Crude Birth Rate, e.g. of Solan is calculated as:

Index value of CBR = $\dfrac{\text{Actual Value of CBR of the district} - \text{Min. Value of CBR in state}}{\text{Max. Value of CBR in the state} - \text{Min. Value of CBR in state}}$

By putting values of crude birth rate of Solan = $\dfrac{19.6-9.0}{20.7-9.0}$ (pl. see table-2)

Index value of CBR of Solan district = 0.91

Step II: Index value of Crude Birth Rate, Crude Death Rate and Under Five Mortality Rate is calculated with the help of above mentioned formula for all the districts of the state.

Step III: Health Status Index is further calculated by subtracting summed up average index value of Crude birth rate, crude death rate and under five mortality rate from 1 individually for all the districts. (Table-6)

Relevant maps, figures, tables are prepared. Arc GIS-9.0 version was also used to prepare maps.

Spatial Pattern of Health Status in terms of Crude Birth Rate, Crude Death Rate and Under Five Mortality Rate in Himachal Pradesh

Health status of any region is mainly determined by crude birth rate, crude death rate, life expectancy at birth, child mortality rate and maternal mortality rate etc.. In the present study spatial patterns of health status in Himachal Pradesh have been examined in terms of index score of crude birth rate, crude death rate and under five mortality rate at district level .

Table Showing District wise Health Status Indicators in Himachal Pradesh

Sr. No.	District	Crude Birth Rate(2010)*	Crude Death Rate (2010)*	Under Five Mortality Rate (2012)**
1.	Solan	19.6	7	33.9
2.	Sirmaur	17.1	4.5	55.5
3.	Shimla	19.7	6	39.3
4.	Mandi	18.1	5.5	23
5.	Lahaul& Spiti	9	5.4	48.6
6.	Kullu	16.9	5	34.9
7.	Kinnaur	11	6	49.5
8.	Kangra	18.7	6.7	59.2
9.	Hamirpur	17.2	7.5	22.1
10.	Chamba	20.7	5.1	54.2
11.	Bilaspur	19.6	5.9	25.7
12.	Una	17.7	7.4	30.8
13.	Himachal Pradesh	17.1	6.1	42.5

Source: * District Wise Statistical Abstract of H.P.,2011 [19]
** Estimates From National demographic and Mortality
Surveys, Published by Lancet Global Health (2013) [8]

Crude birth rate plays a vital role in determining the health status of the population of a region. Low birth rate contributes significantly to promote health status as the limited births considerably not only help in maintaining maternal health but also reducing the pressure on health facilities. Himachal Pradesh had a crude birth rate of only 17.1 per thousand as compared to national average of 22.1 per thousand live births. The main causative factors for low birth rate in Himachal Pradesh are the use of effective family planning measures and high literacy level [20]. The birth rate varies from 20.7 per thousand live births in Chamba

Table Showing District wise Contraceptive Prevalence Rate in
Himachal Pradesh

District/ State	Sterilization	Pill
	Female	
Chamba	33.3	4.2
Kangra	48.8	2
Lahaul& Spiti	34.8	4.7
Kullu	41.8	3.1
Mandi	52.2	2.4
Hamipur	56.5	2.2
Una	48.5	2.6
Bilaspur	54.8	1.3
Solan	48.6	1.2
Sirmaur	54.1	1
Shimla	47.4	0.8
Kinnaur	34.9	0.1
Himachal Pradesh	46.3	2.1

Source: District Level Household Survey, 2007-2008 [21]

to 9 per thousand live births in Lahaul & Spiti district (Fig.-1). This may be attributed to the state's lowest female sterilization (33.3 percent) and lowest female literacy rate in district Chamba (Table-3, 4). In Lahaul & district, though (i) the percentage of sterilized females and (ii) the percentage of male and female literates are low yet the percentage of women having contraceptive pills is the highest in the state. Extremely small size of population associated with Buddhism and the tradition of late marriages in the district may be associated with low birth rates.

The crude death rate of Himachal Pradesh, on other hand, was 6.1 deaths per thousand in 2010 which was less than the national average of 7.2 deaths per thousand of total population. It was so as Himachal Pradesh has made remarkable progress in expansion of health facilities and services [22]. Crude death rate, however, varied between the highest values of 7.5 deaths per thousand population in Hamirpur to the lowest of 4.5 deaths per thousand population in Sirmour (Fig.-1). Age specific death rates and age structure of population, traditions of late marriages can further be explored to understand these variations.

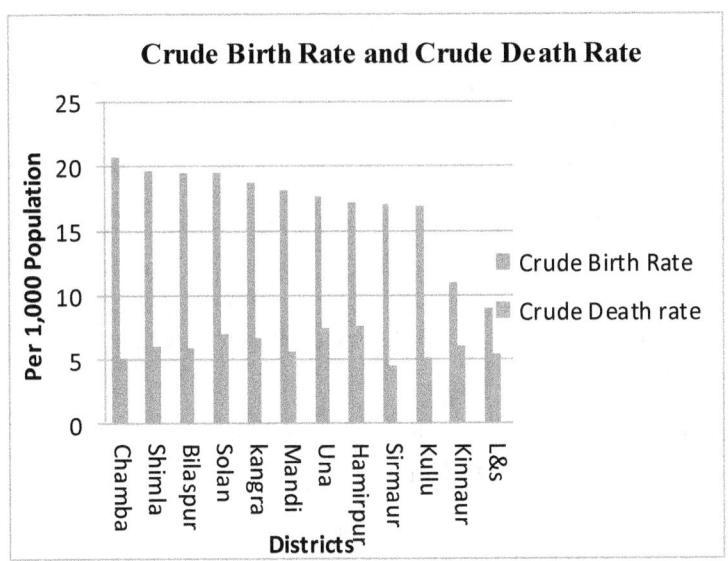

Fig.-1 Source: District Statistical Abstract of H.P., 2011 [19]

Under five mortality (deaths among children up to the age of five years per 1000 live births in a given year), like infant mortality rate, is considered as a sophisticated index of mortality to understand socio- economic development.

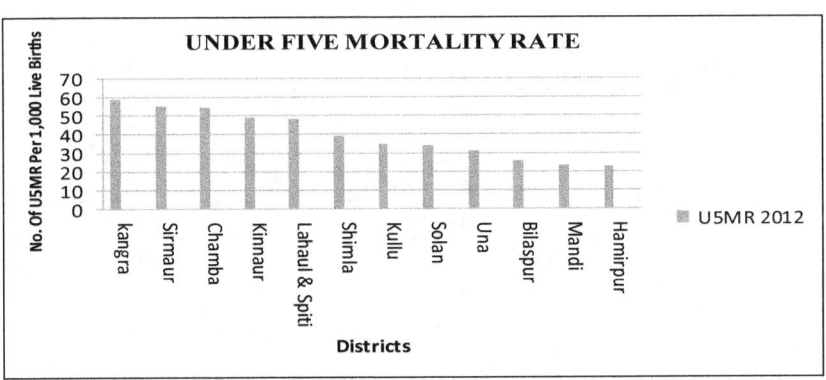

Fig.-2 *Source: Estimates from National Demographic and Mortality Surveys, Published by Lancet Global Health (2013) [8]*

The under five mortality rate in Himachal Pradesh was 49 per thousand live births which was less than the national average of 59 per thousand live births. Himachal Pradesh has made tremendous progress in providing access to safe drinking water and has lowered open defecation rate [23]. The under five mortality rate varied from the highest of 59.2 per 1000 live births in district Kangra to the lowest of 22.2 per thousand live births in district Hamirpur (Fig.-2). There were five districts in the state which had an under five mortality of more than the state average of 42.5 per thousand live births. In these parts of the state, large population, low literacy rate, difficult accessibility to health services distributed to high under five mortality rate (Table-4, 5).

Table Showing District wise Male/Female Literacy Rate in Himachal Pradesh

Sr. No.	District/ State	Male	Female	Total
1.	Himachal Pradesh	90.83	76.6	83.78
2.	Chamba	84.19	62.14	73.19
3.	Kangra	92.55	80.62	86.49
4.	Lahaul& Spiti	86.97	66.5	77.24
5.	Kullu	88.8	71.01	80.14
6.	Mandi	91.51	74.33	82.81
7.	Hamipur	95.28	83.44	89.01
8.	Una	92.75	81.67	87.23
9.	Bilaspur	92.39	78.9	85.67
10.	Solan	91.19	78.02	85.02
11.	Sirmaur	86.76	72.55	79.98
12.	Shimla	90.73	77.8	84.55
13.	Kinnaur	88.37	71.34	80.77

Table Showing District wise Health Infrastructure and Per
Capita Income in Himachal Pradesh

Sr. No.	District	Primary Health Centres (No. of Persons Per PHC)	Per Capita Income (in Rs.)
1.	Lahaul & Spiti	1970.5	83,070
2.	Kinnaur	4014.19	60,513
3.	Shimla	9349.241	46,229
4.	Bilaspur	11236.94	38,788
5.	Chamba	12353.43	25,970
6.	Sirmour	14726.78	36,006
7.	Mandi	16121.26	28,441
8.	Kullu	16825.92	42,023
9.	Solan	16960.88	67,531
10.	Hamirpur	17472.81	36,285
11.	Kangra	18840.29	33,090
12.	Una	27424.05	36,690
13.	Himachal Pradesh	13941	44,553

Source: Planning Commission of H.P., 2005-06. [25]
Directorate of Health Services Shimla, 2011. [26]

For understanding the level of health Status in Himachal Pradesh,
health status index, as explained in methodology is calculated at
district level in 2011-13 (Fig.-3).

Table- 6: Himachal Pradesh: Health Status Index (Data by Districts) (Based on Crude Birth Rate, Crude Death Rate and Under Five Mortality Rate)

District	Index value of CBR	Index value of CDR	Index value of U5MR	Total of Index values	Average of Index values	Index of Health Status	Rank
Bilaspur	0.91	0.47	0.1	1.47	0.49	0.51	5
Chamba	1	0.2	0.87	2.07	0.69	0.31	9
Hamirpur	0.7	1	0	1.7	0.57	0.43	7
Kangra	0.83	0.73	1	2.56	0.85	0.15	11
Kinnaur	0.17	0.5	0.74	1.41	0.47	0.53	4
Kullu	0.68	0.17	0.35	1.19	0.4	0.6	2
Lahaul & Spiti	0	0.3	0.71	1.01	0.34	0.66	1
Mandi	0.78	0.33	0.02	1.14	0.38	0.62	3
Shimla	0.91	0.5	0.46	1.88	0.63	0.37	8
Sirmaur	0.69	0	0.9	1.59	0.53	0.47	6
Solan	0.91	0.83	0.32	2.06	0.69	0.31	9
Una	0.74	0.97	0.23	1.94	0.65	0.35	10

Source: * District Statistical Abstract of H.P.,2011 [19]
** Estimates From National demographic and Mortality Surveys, Published by Lancet Global Health (2013)[8]

There were large variations among districts in terms of index of health status of population in Himachal Pradesh (Table-6). The districts falling in the category of high health status index of more than 0.60 were Lahaul & Spiti, Kullu and Mandi. The districts of Kinnaur, Bilaspur, Sirmaur and Hamirpur all were in medium category of health status index with an index value of between 0.40 and 0.60. The districts included in the low level of health status with an index value of less than 0.40 were the districts of Shimla, Una, Solan, Chamba and Kangra. The lowest level of health status (0.15) was observed in Kangra which accommodated more than twenty percent population of the state and experienced high crude birth rate, high crude death rate and highest under five mortality rate in the state. Lahaul &Spiti with the highest index value of 0.66 of health status was at rank one in the state. It accommodated less than one per cent of the total population of the state. District

Chamba on the other hand, with an extremely low level of health status had the lowest levels of total male and female literacy, lowest rate of contraceptive prevalence and lowest per capita income in the state (Table-3, 4, 5). Kinnaur, Bilaspur, Sirmaur and Hamirpur registered a moderate index of between 0.40 and 0.60 as these were the districts which had moderate percentage of sterilized females and literate females and had lower capita income than the state average. The health status in terms of crude birth rate, crude death rate and under five mortality rate was thus significantly affected by various factors such as levels of total, male and female literacy rates, use of family planning methods, pressure of population , per capita income etc.

Fig.-3: Relationship between Health Status and (i) Environmental Variables; (ii) Availability of Health Services

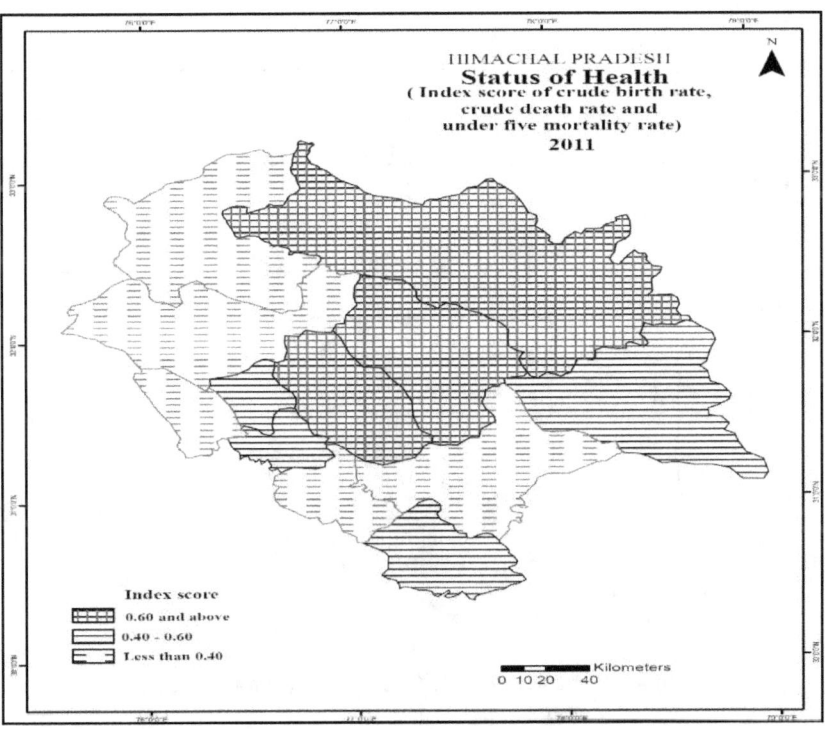

In this study an attempt is also made to understand the relationship between health status and (i) environmental variables i.e. access to safe drinking water and availability of sanitation facilities and (ii) availability of health services i.e. availability of doctors and nurses.

Table Showing District wise Availability of Drinking Water, Sanitation Facilities, Nurses and Doctors in Himachal Pradesh

Sr No.	Districts	Under Five Mortality Rate	Percentage of house-holds with access to safe Drinking water b	Percentage of house-holds with Sanitation facilities b	Nurses per 10,000 population c	Doctors per 10,000 Population c
1	Bilaspur	25.7	90.4	70.6	5.1	2.46
2	Chamba	54.2	88.0	51.5	4.0	1.48
3	Hamirpur	22.1	95.5	89.3	4.5	1.98
4	Kangra	59.2	93.4	65.5	0.9	1.2
5	Kinnaur	49.5	85.6	69.2	3.6	5.46
6	Kullu	34.9	86.8	58.4	6.6	1.81
7	Lahaul & Spiti	48.6	77.0	78.1	8.9	7.3
8	Mandi	23.0	93.2	82.7	1.1	1.44
9	Shimla	39.3	84.9	68.3	3.6	1.47
10	Sirmaur	55.5	79.2	62.1	2.1	2.63
11	Solan	33.9	85.8	73.4	1.3	2.39
12	Una	30.8	93	60.3	2.1	1.23
13	Himachal Pradesh	42.5	89.7	69.1	3.7	2.57

Source: a Estimates From National demographic and Mortality Surveys, Published by Lancet Global Health (2013)[8]

b Census of India, 2011[27]

c Directorate of Health Services Shimla, 2011 [28]

Note: 1. Sources of drinking water include tap water from treated sources, well covered well, hand pump and tube

2. Sanitation facilities include percentage of households having latrine facilities.

Table Showing Correlation between Under Five Mortality
Rate and Environmental Variables and Health Services
Variables

Variables	Co-efficient Value
Access to safe drinking water	-0.51
Availability of Sanitation facilities	-0.54
Availability of Doctors (Per 10,000 persons)	0.085
Availability of Nurses (per 10,000 Persons)	-0.020

Source: Estimates From National demographic and
Mortality Surveys, Published by Lancet Global Health
(2013)[8] Census of India, 2011[27], Directorate of Health
Services Shimla,2011 [28]

Water and sanitation are integral aspects of good human health.
Safe water and improved sanitation lower the risk of many diseases
and keep people healthy. Results indicated that environmental
factors such as access to safe drinking water and availability of
sanitation facilities played a much more important role than
availability of health services like availability of doctors and
availability of nurses in controlling under five mortality. Access to
safe drinking water was negatively and moderately (-0.51) related
with the under five mortality rate in the state and an areal
correspondence of 0.66 was observed between them (Table-8),
(Fig.-4). As far as the supply of safe drinking water is concerned, as
per the statistics available, about ninety per cent of the households
in the state had this facility (Table-7). In spite of a good percentage
of households privileged with this facility, the supply of clean and
safe drinking water was, however, irregular and restricted on many
occasions (Plates-1,2,3),[29][30][31].

Not only this, clean and safe drinking water was not adequately
available to the people in far flung areas who were forced to drink
polluted water from khuds (Plate-5), [32]. Due to old sewerage,
drain water percolates into water pipes (Plate-4),[31] and people are
forced to consume contaminated water during the periods of crisis.

Moreover, the traditional sources of water are not cleaned properly and regularly (Plate-6), [33]. In severe winters the situation worsens as water freezes in water pipes and people use traditional and unclean sources of water. Spread of diseases like diarrhoea, viral fever etc. is quite common among people using water from these sources and hundreds of people have been infected in the past few years [34]. It can, therefore, be concluded that it is not only the access to safe drinking water which is important, but also the regularity and frequency with which the safe water is distributed among the population. Availability of sanitation facilities, however had a greater effect on under five mortality rate in the state as a co-efficient value of -0.54 was recorded between the two variables and the degree of areal correspondence was, however, only 0.58 (Table-8), (Fig.-5).

Fig.-4   Fig. 5

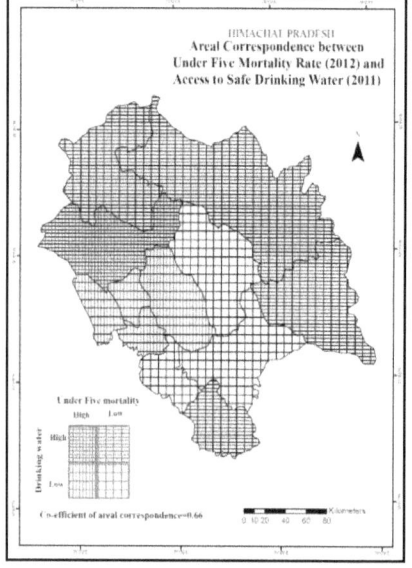

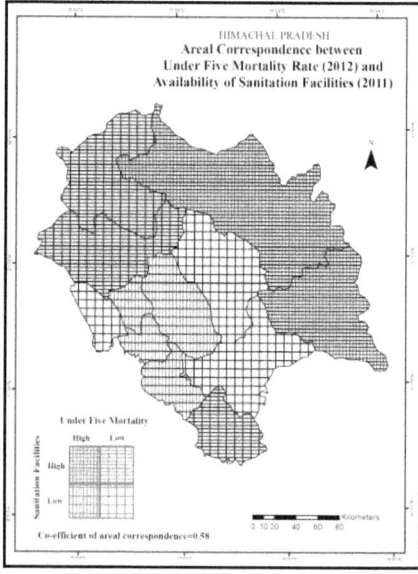

Table Showing District wise Areal Correspondence between Health Status and Environmental Variables and Health Services Variables in HP

Districts	Under five mortality rate*	Access to Safe Drinking Water**	Availablity of Sanitation Facilities**	Availablity of Doctors***	Availability of Nurses***
Chamba	High	Low	Low	Low	High
Kangra	High	High	Low	Low	Low
Lahul& Spiti	High	Low	High	High	High
Kinnaur	High	Low	High	High	Low
Sirmaur	High	Low	low	low	Low
Hamirpur	Low	High	High	Low	High
Bilaspur	Low	High	High	Low	High
Una	Low	High	Low	Low	Low
Mandi	Low	High	High	Low	Low
Shimla	Low	Low	Low	High	Low
Solan	Low	Low	High	Low	Low
Kullu	Low	Low	Low	Low	High

Source: * Estimates From National demographic and Mortality Surveys, Published by Lancet Global Health (2013)[8]
** Census of India, 2011[27]
*** Directorate of Health Services Shimla 2011 [28]

It may be mentioned here that the status of health in Himachal Pradesh which is significantly determined by access to safe drinking water and availability of sanitation facilities also needs to be studied in the context of availability of doctors and nurses (Table-9) (Fig.-6). The coefficient values of correlation between under five mortality and availability of doctors (per 10,000 persons) and availability of nurses (per 10,000 persons) were 0.085 and -0.020 respectively. Such an observation puts a question mark on the utilisation of these resources in the state. Himachal Pradesh is, no doubt, much better than many other states in the country in terms of availability of doctors and nurses but utilization of these health services in different districts in the state may suffer due to difficult terrain insufficient and inefficient means of transportation, uneven distribution of health services, shortage of staff, shortage of facilities etc. Such a situation may delay the meeting objective of 'Health for All'. (Plate-7, 8, 9, 10,)[36], [37][38][39][40][41].

Micro level studies may also be conducted to have an in-depth understanding of the relationship between availability of doctors and nurses and the utilisation of these services.

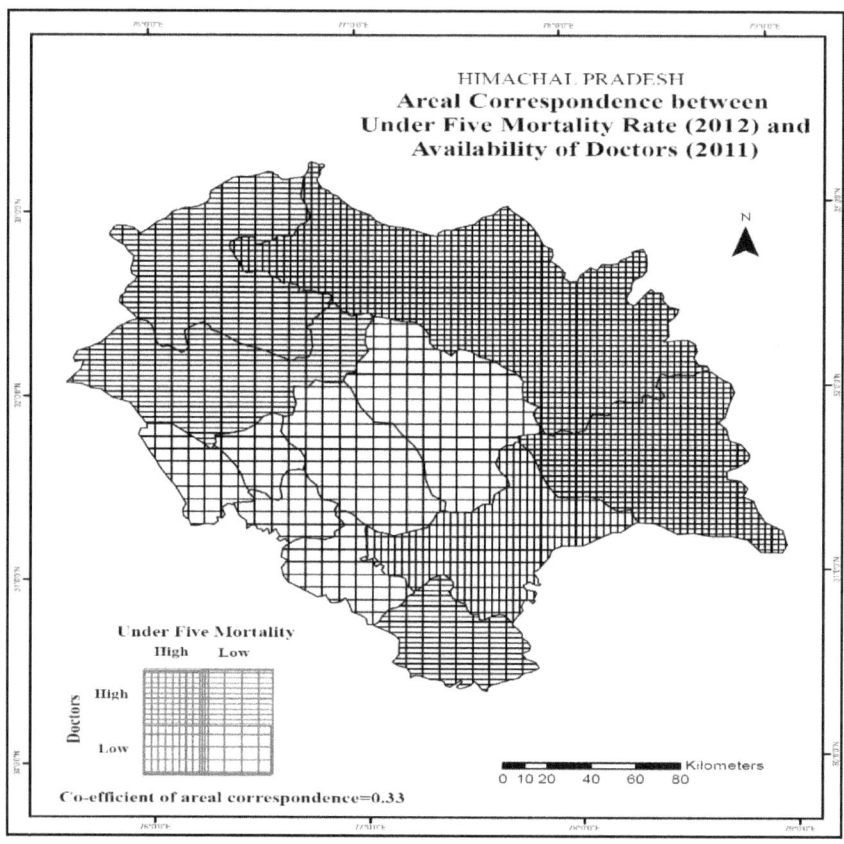

Fig.-6: *Showing Areal Correspondence between Under five Mortality rate*

Impact of shortage: Illustrations:

Plate Showing No Wards to Admit patients in Hospital in Palampur (District Kangra)

Plate Showing Long queue in OPD of the Hospital (District Kangra)

In order to study health status in Himachal Pradesh health status index was devised with the help of crude birth rate, crude death rate and under five mortality rate by giving due weightage to the highest and lowest values of these indicators. Marked inter-district variations in health status were observed. District Lahaul & Spiti had the highest level of health status in the state as it had tradition of late marriages; highest rate of contraceptive prevalence; highest per capita income; lowest density of population in the state. On the other hand, district Chamba had an extremely low level of health status with lowest contraceptive prevalence, lowest literacy levels and lowest per capita income in the state. The health status in terms of crude birth rate, crude death rate and under five mortality rate was significantly affected by various factors such as levels of male and female literacy rate, use of family planning methods, pressure of population and per capita income.

A moderate effect of environmental variables i.e. drinking water and sanitation facilities on health status was observed in the state. The availability of health services (i.e. doctors and nurses) was however not found to be very effective in controlling mortality particularly under five mortality rate. The utilisation of health facilities made available by the government needs to be promoted by adequate, good and efficient means of transportation. Regular and adequate access to safe drinking water needs to be given top priority for achieving good health status in all parts of the state.

References:

1. World Health organization, Chronicle of the world health organization, WHO, Interim Commission, Vol.-1, No.-1-2, 1948.
2. World Health Organisation, Health and Development, http://www.who.int/hdp/en/
3. Pathak, P., Composite Index-Based Approach for Analysis of the Health System in the Indian Context", IIHMR, Working Paper No. 2, 1992, 1-28.
4. Lincoln Chen, Timothy Evans, Sudhir Anand, Jo Ivey Boufford, Hilary Brown, Mushtaque
5. Chowdhury, Marcos Cueto, Lola Dare, Gilles Dussault, Gijs Elzinga, Elizabeth Fee, Demissie Habte, Piya Hanvoravongchai, Marian Jacobs, Christoph Kurowski, Sarah Michael, Ariel Pablos-Mendez, Nelson Sewankambo, Giorgio Solimano, Barbara Stilwell, Alex de Waal and Suwit Wibulpolprasert, Human resources for health: overcoming the crisis , Lancet, 364, 2004,1984–90.
6. Sudhir Anand and Till Barnighausen, Human resources and health outcomes: cross-country econometric study, Lancet, 364, 2004, 1603–09.
7. Niko Speybroeck,Yohannes Kinfu, Mario R. Dal Poz and David B. Evans, Reassessing the relationship between human resources for health, intervention coverage and health outcomes, World Health Organization Geneva, March, 2000.
8. Neeru Gupta,Blerta Maliqi,Adson Franca,Frank Nyonator, Muhammad A Pate, David Sanders ,Hedia Belhadj and

Bernadette Daelmans, Human resources for maternal, newborn and child health: from measurementand planning to performance for improved health outcomes, Human Resources for Health, , 9:16, 2011, 9-16.

9. Unicef, Infant and Child Mortality in India: Levels trends and determinants, National Institute of Medical Statistics, Indian Council of Medical Research,1-23
http://www.unicef.org

10. Leo s. Morales, Raynard s. Kington and Robert o. Valdez , Socioeconomic, cultural, and behavioural factors affecting Hispanic health outcomes, J Health Care Poor Underserved, 13(4), 2002,477–503.

11. Mostafa H., Socioeconomic differentials in mortality by cause of death. Health Services Reports, 88, May 1973, 449-456.

12. Mahesh Patel, Effects of the health service and environmental factors on infant mortality: the case of Sri Lanka, Journal of Epidemiology and Community Health, 34, 1980, 76-82.

13. Govil, D. and Purohit, N., Health Care System, in Rout, H. (eds.) Health Care System- A Global Survey, (New Century Publications, Delhi 2012),577-611.

14. Sample Registration System, SRS bulletein, Registrar General of India, 46(1), 2011, 1-6.

15. Ram U, Jha P, Ram F, Kumar K, Awasthi S, Shet A, Pader J, Nansukusa and S, Kumar R. Neonatal, 1-59 month, and under-5 mortality in 597 Indian districts, 2001 to 2012: estimates from national demographic and mortality surveys. Lancet Global Health 2013; Published online September 19, 2013.

16. Census of India, Population totals, http://www.censusindia.gov.in/2011

17. M.H. Suryanarayana, Ankush Agarwal and K. Seeta prabhu, Inequality- adjusted human development index for india's states, UNDP India Report, 2011, http://www.in.undp.org/

18. Reddy, K. N. and V. Selvaraju, Determinants of health status in India: An empirical investigation, The 76th Annual Conference Volume of The Indian Economic Association, Indira gandhi institute of development research, Bombay, 1994.

19. Dadibhavi, R. V and S. T. Bagalkoti, Inter-state disparities in health status in India, Yojana, 38(23), 1994.

20. Govt. of Himachal Pradesh, District statistical abstract, Economic & Statistics Department, 2011, http:// admis.hp.nic.in.

21. S N Gupta, N Ahmed and S Gupta, Slowly rising population hilly population of himachal: A step towards stabilization, Medical Health Science Research, 3(3), 2013, 385-390.

22. Health and Family Welfare, District Level Household and Facility Survey (DLHS-3) 2007- 08, International Institute for Population Sciences (IIPS), 2010, Himachal Pradesh, Mumbai.

23. National Health Profile, Health Infrastructure, Central Bureau of Health Intelligence, Directorate General of Health Services,2011 Govt. of India, www.cbhidghs.nic.in., 184-230.

24. Government of India, India human development Report, Institute of Applied Manpower Research Planning Commission, 2011,1-403

25. Census of India 2011, Series-3, Provisional Population Totals, http://www.censusindia.gov.in/2011

26. Govt. of Himachal Pradesh, Planning Commision, 2005-06, http://hpplanning.nic.in/Directorate of Health Services, Directory of medical and Public health institutions in Himachal Pradesh, Department of Health and Family Welfare of H.P, 2011.

27. Census of India, House listing and Housing Census Data Highlights – 2011; Houses, Household Amenities and Assets-, 2011.

28. Directorate of Health Services, Staff Position, Department of Health and Family Welfare of H.P., 2011.

29. Kiran Deep, 50 years of promises and lies in Bilaspur, The Tribune, May 3, 2006.

30. Shalender Singh, Nahan facing acute water shortage, NVO News, 2010, August 31, http://nvonews.com/

31. Water supply partially restored in Palampur, The Tribune, July 1, 2007.

32. Rakesh Lohumi, Rs 162-cr plan to replace old sewerage in Shimla, The Tribune, April 21, 2010.

33. Shalender Singh, Villages made to consume polluted water in Himachal, NVO,News, May 1, 2009

34. Gauri basant Sharma, Himachal Pradesh and its neglected water resources, Hp Hill Post 2011,http://hillpost.in/

35. Dharam Prakash Gupta, 666 traditional water sources rejuvenated, The Tribune, April 4, 2010.

36. The Tribune, Chamba areas lack health services Chamba, The Tribune, May 1, 2008.
37. Kuldeep Chauhan, Docs' shortage ails hospitals in Mandi, The Tribune, February 3, 2011.
38. Kuldeep Chauhan, Mandi zonal hospital lacks basic facilities, The Tribune, March 7, 2012.
39. Ravinder Sood, Ailing' Palampur hospital looks up to govt., The Tribune, October 14, 2009.
40. Kangra hospital victim of govt apathy, The Tribune, January 19, 2008.
41. Planning Commission, Himachal Pradesh Development Report, New Delhi, Government of India, 2002, 155-178.

Chapter-VIII
Bioremedial impact of Withania Somnifera on Arsenic induced Testicular Toxicity in Charles Foster Rats

Md. Samiur Rahman*

Abstract

The objective of this study was to observe the ameliorative effect of Withania somnifera on arsenic induced testicular toxicity. In the present study, arsenic in the form of sodium arsenite was administered orally to male Charles Foster rats for 45 days. It caused the decrease in the sperm counts, sperm motility accompanied by an increased incidence of sperm abnormalities and hormonal imbalance leading to infertility. Thereafter, ethanolic root extract of Withania somnifera was administered for 30 days to observe its ameliorative effect on male reproductive system. The study reveals that after the administration of W.somnifera, there was significant reversal in the parameters denotes that it not only possesses antioxidant and rejuvenating property but it also helps in maintaining the cellular integrity of testicular cells leading to normal functioning of it. So it can be promoted as one of the best antidotes against arsenic induced reproductive toxicity.

Keywords: *Sodium arsenite, W. somnifera, Testicular toxicity, Sperm Count, Testosterone*

Junior Research Fellow, Mahavir Cancer Institute & Research Centre, Patna, Bihar

Introduction

Millions of people worldwide are at risk for the development of cardiovascular disease, diabetes, cancer and other adverse health effects from drinking arsenic-contaminated groundwater. Chronic exposure to arsenic affect organ systems like skin, liver, developing fetus, cardiovascular, pulmonary, nervous, endocrine, reproductive, hematological and immunological systems in the human body. In context of male reproductive endocrinology the sodium arsenite directly alters the spermatogenesis and testosterone level. *In Vivo* transition of inorganic arsenic into the organic form causes the release of free radicals which in turn promote endocrine disruption which led to high secretion of luteinising hormone (LH) leading to improper functioning of the leydig cells. The extreme low levels of testosterone cause abnormal functioning of the spermatogenesis.

Withania somnifera also called as Ashwagandha is an important medicinal herb in Ayurveda and indigenous medical systems. Well known for its anti-inflammatory (Begum and Sadique, 2004), antioxidant (Dhuley, 1998), antitumor (Jayaprakasam *et al.*, 2003), antistress (Vaishali *et al.*, 1987), antiulcer (Bhatnagar *et al.*, 2005), adaptogenic (Bhattacharya and Muruganandam, 2003), immunomodulatory (Rasool and Varalakshmi, 2006) and rejuvenating properties (Kumar *et al.*, 2013; Patil *et al.*, 2012). In the traditional medicine, especially in Ayurveda as Rasayana *W.somnifera* is used as rejuvenating tonic (Sukh, 2005; API, 2001; Upton, 2000) and male reproductive booster (Shukla *et al.*, 2011).

However, no studies have been reported the effect of *W.somnifera* root extract as antidote against arsenic induced male reproductive toxicity in rats. Thus, the present study deciphers the ameliorative effect of *W.somnifera* against arsenic induced testicular toxicity.

Materials & Methods
Test Chemical: Sodium Arsenite (98.5%) manufactured by Biosol Laboratories Pvt. Limited, Kolkata, India was obtained from the Scientific store of Patna.

Animals: Charles Foster rats (30 males), weighing 160g to 180g of 8 weeks old, were obtained from animal house of Mahavir Cancer Institute and Research Centre, Patna, India (CPCSEA Regd-No. 1129/bc/07/CPCSEA). The research work was approved by the IAEC (Institutional Animal Ethics Committee) with IAEC No. IAEC/2012/12/04. Food and water to rats were provided *ad libitum* (prepared mixed formulated food by the laboratory itself). The experimental animals were housed in conventional polypropylene cages in small groups (2 each). The rats were randomly assigned to control and treatment groups. The temperature in the experimental animal room was maintained at 22 ± 2^0C with 12 h light/dark cycle.

Preparation of plant ethanolic extract: In the present study, dry root of *W.somnifera* were purchased from Haridwar Medicinal Store, Haridwar, Uttrakahand, India. The identity of the medicinal plant was confirmed by Dr. Ramakant Pandey (Botanist), Department of Biochemistry, Patna University, Patna, Bihar, India. The collected roots of *W. somnifera* were shade dried and were grinded into the fine powder. The powder was then soaked in 70% ethanol for 48 hours and finally extracted with 5% absolute ethanol using soxhlet apparatus for 6 -8 hours and the residue was concentrated and dried at 37^0C. The ethanolic extract dose was calculated after LD_{50} estimation and finally made to 120 mg kg^{-1} body weight.

Experimental Design: In the present study, arsenic in the form of sodium arsenite was administered orally to male Charles Foster rats (n = 24) at the dose of 8 mg Kg^{-1} body weight per day for 60 days while control male rats (n = 6) were also taken for the comparative study. Thereafter, ethanolic root extract of *Withania somnifera* (Ashwagandha) was prepared and administered at the dose of 120 mg Kg^{-1} body weight per day for 30 days to observe the ameliorative effect of it on male reproductive system. Drinking water and feed was provided to the animal *ad libitum*. After the end of the experiment the rats were anaesthesized and their sperm counts were done and then they were sacrificed and their serum was extracted for serum for lipid peroxidation study, Luteinising hormone and testosterone hormone assay while their testes were fixed in the neutral formalin for histopathological study.

Sperm counts: The Cauda epididymis was dissected out and washed thoroughly in normal Saline (0.85 %). Cauda epididymis was incised and made puncture at several places in 1 ml of distilled water in watch glass so as to allow the sperm to ooze out. After that, two drops of Eosin Y was mixed well with sperm. Sperm counts was made using an improved Neubauer's chamber taking a drop of above preparation in it & observed at 450x magnification.

Sperm motility: Cauda epididymis was dissected out and ruptured on microscopic slide. After covering it with a cover slip, the motility of the spermatozoa was examined.

Hormonal Assay: Using the ELISA method Luteinising Hormone (LH) & Testosterone kit of LILAC Medicare (P) Ltd., Mumbai was utilized for the experiment. The normal range was calibrated and then 25 µl serum samples were taken in the microwell plates. 100 µl of enzyme conjugate was added in each well. After that, it was left for incubation at $37^\theta C$ in incubator for 1 hour. Then, the wells were washed with 300 µl distilled water for at least 3 times and blotted. Then, 100 µl TMB solution was added as substrate in each well plate and was again left for the incubation for 15 minutes for the colour. Finally, 100 µl stop solution was added in each well to stop the reaction. Reading was taken at 630nm through Merck ELISA reader in ng/ml value.

Lipid Peroxidation: Thiobarbituric acid reactive substances (TBARS), as a marker for LPO, were determined by the double heating method (Draper and Hadley, 1990). The principle of the method was a spectrophotometric measurement of the colour produced during the reaction to thiobarbituric acid (TBA) with malondialdehyde (MDA). For this purpose, 2.5 ml of 100 g/l trichloroacetic acid (TCA) solution was added to 0.5 ml serum in a centrifuge tube and incubated for 15 min at $90^\theta C$. After cooling in tap water, the mixture was centrifuged at 3000 g for 10 min, and 2 ml of the supernatant was added to 1 ml of 6.7 g/l TBA solution in a test-tube and again incubated for 15 min at 90^{0}C. The solution was then cooled in tap water and its absorbance was measured using Thermo Scientific UV-10 (UV –Vis) spectrophotometer (USA) at 532 nm.

Histopathology: All rats were sacrificed after the scheduled period. A midsaggital incision was made and testicular tissue from all the rats were removed and fixed in 10% neutral formalin. For the light microscopic study the Haematoxylin-Eosin stained slides were prepared and the sections were viewed under light microscope.

Statistical Analysis: Results are presented as mean ± SD and total variation present in a set of data was analysed through one way analysis of variance (ANOVA). Difference among mean values has been analysed by applying Dunnett's test. Calculations were performed with the Graph Pad Prism Program (Graph Pad software, Inc., San Diego, U.S.A.). The criterion for statistical significance was set at $P< 0.05$.

Results

Morbidity & Mortality : The rats after 60 days arsenic exposure (8mg Kg^{-1} body weight) have shown signs of toxicity such as nausea, nose bleeding, lack of body co-ordination (11 percent of rats showed paralysis like symptoms), blackening of tongue and foot and general body weakness.

Sperm counts: The sodium arsenite treated rats caused marked reduction in their sperm counts in comparison to control ones. But, after the administration of W.somnifera there was significant increase in the sperm counts denotes normalisation in the testicular functioning (Table.1.).

Sperm morphology & motility: The sodium arsenite treated rats caused marked reduction in their sperm motility in comparison to control ones (Table.2.). The major sperm abnormalities observed were loss of sperm tails, coiling in sperm tails etc. denotes the degeneration caused by sodium arsenite. But, after the administration of *W.somnifera* there was significant increase in the sperm motility denotes restoration in the spermatozoa.

Hormonal Assay: The decreased level of serum testosterone after arsenic exposure in comparison to control denotes the endocrine disruption. While there is significant increase in its level after administration of *W.somnifera* denotes the normalisation of the endocrine function (Table.3.) Whereas, there is an increase in the LH levels after arsenic exposure in comparison to control but there is decrease in the LH levels ($p < 0.001$) after administration of *W.somnifera* (Table. 4.).

Lipid peroxidation Assay: There is increase in the lipid peroxidation levels after arsenicexposure in comparison to control denotes the cellular oxidative stress but after the administration of *W.somnifera* there is significant decrease in the LPO levels denotes the antioxidant property of *W.somnifera* (Table.5.).

Histopathological study: The control testis shows normal architecture of seminiferous tubules (ST) with well arranged spermatogenetic stages – primary spermatocytes (PS), spermatogonia (SG), spermatids (SPM) and spermatozoa. The leydig cells in the inter–seminiferous tubular space are normal in architecture denotes the normal functioning of the spermatogenesis (Fig.1.). But, in sodium arsenite treated testicular sections, it has caused severe damage to the testicular cells. There are seminiferous tubules with no spermatogenetic stages or if are present, only 5% denotes the normal functioning of it. The leydig cells, also appears to be in highly degenerative condition as haemorrhage in them can be observed (Fig.2 & 3). But, after the administration of *W.somnifera* there has been immense amelioration, as restoration in the spermatogenetic stages can be observed. The primary spermatocytes (PS), spermatogonia (SG), spermatids (SPM) and spermatozoa all are well arranged denotes the significant normalisation in the function of the testicular cells. The leydig cell also shows amelioration denotes the normalisation in its function (Fig.4.).

Discussion:

In the present work, the sodium arsenite (8mg Kg^{-1} body weight) has caused severe damage to the male reproductive function. The decreased levels of sperm counts, sperm motility, testosterone levels and lipid peroxidation represent the arsenic induced toxicity. It also promoted degeneration in sperm morphology and complete arrest of spermatogenetic stages which leads to infertility. *W.somnifera* is thought to be amphoteric and can help in regulating the important physiological processes. It ameliorate the male reproductive function by acting as an antioxidant, with its active constituents sitoindosides VII-X and withaferin that decreases the levels of lipid peroxidation (Ahmad *et al.*, 2010; Bhatnagar *et al.*, 2005; Gupta *et al.*, 2003; Bhattacharya *et al.*, 2001; Bhattacharya *et al.*, 1997). When there is an excess of a certain hormone, the plant-based hormone precursor occupies cell membrane receptor sites in such a way that the actual hormone cannot attach and exert its effect normalising the hormonal activity (Ilayperuma *et al.*, 2002; Abdel-Magied *et al.*, 2001). Thus, in this study, the LH & Testosterone levels were normalised by the receptor based function of *W.somnifera* extract.

W.somnifera administration shows a major reversal in the testicular function as there was spermatogenetic stages were restored. This denotes the rejuvenating activity of *W.somnifera* in testicular cells. Thus, from the present study, we can concluded that *W.somnifera* is a novel drug which not only possesses antioxidant and rejuvenating property but also maintains the cellular integrity of testicular cells leading to normal functioning of it. It should be one of the drugs which can be used as an antidote against arsenic induced reproductive toxicity.

References

1). Abdel-Magied EM, Abdel-Rahman HA, Harraz FM. (2001). The effect of aqueous extracts of Cynomorium coccineum and Withania somnifera on testicular development in immature Wistar rats. J Ethnopharmacol 75, 1-4.

2). Ahmad MK, Mahdi AA, Shukla KK, Islam N, Rajender S, Madhukar D, Shankhwar SN, Ahmad S. (2010). Withania somnifera improves semen quality by regulating reproductive hormone levels and oxidative stress in seminal plasma of infertile males. Fertil Steril 94(3), 989-96.

3). API: The Ayurvedic Pharmacopoeia of India (2001). Part I, Volume I, 1st edition. New Delhi (India): Government of India, Ministry of Health and Family Welfare, Department of Indian Systems of Medicine & Homoeopathy.

4). Begum V.H. and Sadique J. (2004). Effect of Withania somnifera on glycosaminoglycan synthesis in carrageen in-induced air pouch granuloma. Biochem. Med. Metab. Biol. 38 (3), 272-277.

5). Bhatnagar M, Sisodia SS, Bhatnagar R. (2005). Antiulcer and antioxidant activity of Asparagus racemosa WILLD and Withania somnifera DUNAL in rats. Ann N Y Acad Sci. 1056, 261-278.

6). Bhattacharya SK, Satyan KS, Ghosal S. (1997). Antioxidant activity of glycowithanolides from Withania somnifera. Indian J Exp Biol. 35, 236-239.

7). Bhattacharya A, Ghosal S, Bhattacharya SK. (2001). Anti-oxidant effect of Withania somnifera glycowithanolides in chronic footshock stress induced perturbations of oxidative free radical scavenging enzymes and lipid peroxidation in rat frontal cortex and striatum. J Ethnopharmacol. 74, 1-6.

8). Bhattacharya S.K., Muruganandam AV. (2003). Adaptogenic activity of Withania somnifera: an experimental study using a rat model of chronic stress. Pharmacol. Biochem. Behav. 75(3), 47-555.

9). Dhuley JN. (1998). Effect of Ashwagandha on lipid peroxidation in stress-induced animals. J Ethnopharmacol 60(2), 173-178.

10). Draper HH and Hadley M. (1990). Malondialdehyde determination as index of lipid peroxidation. Methods Enzymol. 186, 421- 31.

11). Gupta SK, Dua A, Vohra BP. (2003). Withania somnifera (ashwagandha) attenuates antioxidant defense in aged spinal cord and inhibits copper induced lipid peroxidation and protein oxidative modifications. Drug Metabol Drug Interact 19, 211-222.

12). Ilayperuma I, Ratnasooriya WD, Weerasooriya TR. (2002). Effect of Withania somnifera root extract on the sexual behaviour of male rats. Asian J Androl 4, 295-298.

13). Jayaprakasam B., Zhang Y., Seeram N.,Nair M. (2003). Growth inhibition of tumor cell lines by withanolides from Withania somnifera leaves. Life Sci. 74(1), 125-132.

14). Kumar A, Ali M, Kumar R, Suman S, Kumar H, Nath, A, Singh JK. and Kumar D. (2013). Withania somnifera protects the haematological alterations caused by Sodium arsenite in Charles foster rats. Int. J. Res. Ayurveda Pharm. 4(4), 491-494.

15). Patil RB, Vora SR and Pillai MM. (2012). Protective effect of spermatogenic activity of Withania Somnifera (Ashwagandha) in galactose stressed mice. Annals of Biological Research 3(8), 4159-4165.

16). Rasool M., Varalakshmi P. (2006). Immunomodulatory role of Withania somnifera root powder on experimental induced inflammation: An in vivo and in vitro study. Vascul.Pharmacol. 44(6), 406-410.

17). Shukla KK., Mahdi AA., Mishra V., Rajender S., Sankhwar SN, Patel D and Das M. (2011). Withania somnifera improves semen quality by combating oxidative stress and cell death and improving essential metal concentrations. Reproductive BioMedicine Online 22, 421– 427.

18). Sukh Dev. (2005). Prime Ayurvedic Plant Drugs. Tunbridge Wells (UK): Anshan.

19). Upton R, editor. (2000). American Herbal Pharmacopoeia and Therapeutic Compendium: Ashwagandha Root (Withania somnifera) – Standards of Analysis, Quality Control, and Therapeutics. Santa Cruz (CA): American Herbal Pharmacopoeia.

20). Vaishali ND, Nilima UR, Dhar HL. (1987). Evaluation of antistress activity of Withania somnifera. Indian journal of clinical Biochemistry 2, 101-108.

Chapter-IX

Phytoremedial effect of Pterocarpus santalinus against Arsenic induced toxicity in Rats

Gautam Anand*

Abstract

The experiment was carried out on Charles Foster rats in which, the rats were exposedorally with sodium arsenite at a very high dose of 80 mg/kg body weight per day for 21 days. The sodium arsenite pre-treated rats were then administered crude aqueous extract of Pterocarpus santalinus at the dose of 300 mg/kg body weight per day through oral administration. The sodium arsenite exposure caused severe hematological alterations in rats showing the unexpected increase in RBCs and WBCs counts but there was significant decrease in blood platelets counts and hemoglobin percentage as compared with control. Under the Liver function test and Kidney function test, Bilirubin level and Alkaline phosphatase level showed abnormal values than the normal range, urea level was significantly higher than the normal range, uric acid was seen lower than the normal range and no effect in creatinine value. Glucose test did not showed much effect on glucose level in the body in comparison to control. Amelioration through Pterocarpus santalinus was observed successively through the biochemical assays and as well as hematological parameters. The overall study reveals that the amelioration by P. Santalinus were achieved successively.

Key words: Sodium arsenite, Pterocarpus santalinus, antidote.

*Project Assistant, Mahavir Cancer Institute & Research Centre, Patna, Bihar

Introduction

Arsenic (As) was firstly documented by "AlbertusMagnus" in 1250, is one of the element having atomic number 33 and atomic mass 74.92, occurs in many minerals, usually in conjunction with Sulpher and metals and also as a pure elemental crystal. [1] Inorganic forms of arsenic are more toxic than organic forms. The trivalent formsare more toxic and react with thiol groups, while pentavalent forms are less toxic.[2] Very few organ systems escape the toxic effects of Arsenic.Trivalent inorganic arsenic inhibits pyruvate dehydrogenase by binding to the sulphydryl groups of dihydrolipoamide. Consequently, conversion of pyruvate to acetyl coenzyme A(CoA) is decreased and citric acid cycle activity is decreased and production of cellular ATP is also decreased.[3][4] Trivalent arsenic inhibits cellular glucose uptake, gluconeogenesis, fatty acid oxidation and further production of glutathione, which prevents cellular oxidative damage.[5] Arsenic is listed as a presumed carcinogenic substance based on the increased prevalence of lung and skin cancer observed in human populations with multiple exposures (primarily through industrial inhalation)[6].

Red Sandelwood or Rakt Chandan is a species of Pterocarpus native to India also known as *"Pterocarpus santalinus"* [7]. It is only found in south India in Kadapa, Chittoor, mostly in the hilly region of Nepal, Pakistan and Srilanka. It is a light demanding small tree growing to 8m tall with a trunk 50-150 cm diameter. It is not frost tolerant, being killed by temperatures of -1°C. The leaves are alternate, 3-9cm long, trifoliate with three leaflets. The flowers are produced in short recemes. The fruit is a pod 6-9cm long containing one or two seeds [8] [9] [10].

In the present study, antidote effect of *Pterocarpus santalinus* was evaluated on arsenic induced toxicity in Charles foster rats to observe its efficacy.

Materials and Methods:

Animals

Charles Foster rats (n=18), under the selected weight range of 150g to 200g were obtained from animal house of Mahavir Cancer Institute and Research Centre, Patna, India (CPCSEA Regd-No. 1129/bc/07/CPCSEA). The research work was approved by the IAEC (Institutional Animal Ethics Committee) with IAEC No. IAEC/2012/12/04. Food and water to rats were provided *ad libitum* (prepared mixed formulated food by the laboratory itself). The experimental model were grouped in to two (n=2) and kept in conventional polypropylene cages. The temperature in the experimental animal room was maintained at 22 ± 2^0C with 12 h light/dark cycle.The rats were randomly assigned to control and treatment groups.

Chemicals:

Sodium Arsenite (98.5%) manufactured by Biosol Laboratories Pvt. Limited, Kolkata, India was obtained from the Scientific store of Patna.

Experimental Design:

Preparation of *Pterocarpus santalinus* aqueous extract: The seeds of *P. santalinus* (Rakt Chandan seeds) were dried thoroughly by using a normal oven in the laboratory or by hot air oven on the particular specified temperature. Crushed completely the dried seeds by using grinders and mortar and pistal to get a fine powdery extracts. The extracted powder was then weighed and dose at the rate of 300mg/kg body weight was made. The prepared aqueous antidote of *P.santalinus* was administered to arsenic induced rats according to their body weight.

Treatment Protocol:

The selected experimental rats were separated in three groups. Group one (1) marked as control group (n=6) to which no treatment was given and to the rest two groups (n=12), Sodium Arsenite at the dose of 80mg/kg body weight was administered orally daily for 21 days.

Upon the sodium arsenite pretreated rats, *Pterocarpus santalinus* seed aqueous extracts were administered at the dose of 300mg/kg body weight orally daily for 45 days. After the each treatment rats were sacrificed and their blood samples were collected for biochemical assessments.

Biochemical Study:

The Liver Function Test (LFT) as Serum Glutamic Pyruvate Transaminase (SGPT) and Serum Glutamic Oxaloacetate Transaminase (SGOT) were measured according to method [11], Alkaline Phosphate (ALP) by method [12] while total bilirubin activity by method [13]. The Kidney Function Test (KFT) were assayed by methods as Urea by [14, 15], Uric acid by [16] and Creatinine by [17].

Statistical Analysis:

Results are presented as mean ± SD and total variation present in a set of data was analysed through one way analysis of variance (ANOVA). Difference among mean values has been analysed by applying Dunnett's t-test. Calculations were performed with the Graph Pad Prism Program (Graph Pad software, Inc., San Diego, U.S.A.). The criterion for statistical significance was set at $P< 0.05$.

Results:

The Arsenic exposed rats at the dose of 80mg/kg body weight for 21 days showed toxicity symptoms such as nausea, nose bleeding, eye irritation and eye discoloration, hair fall, loss of body co-ordination (30% of rats exhibited paralysis like symptoms) and high rate of general body weakness. The Sodium arsenite exposure caused severe hematological alterations in rats showing the unexpected increase in RBCs and WBCs counts but there was significant decrease in blood platelets counts and hemoglobin percentage as compared with control. The Liver function test and Kidney function test showed abnormal increased levels of bilirubin, alkaline phosphatase and urea levels in comparison to control values. Uric acid showed extreme lower levels than the normal range and no abnormal effects in creatinine levels and glucose levels was observed in comparison to control levels. Amelioration through *Pterocarpus santalinus* was the significant study. The biochemical study showed significant amelioration in comparison to control levels (Table- 1).

Table 1. Showing Haematological and Biochemical assay

Diagnostic Parameters	Control (n=6)	Arsenic Treated rats (80mg/kg b.w.)	*P. santalinus* administered rats (300mg/kg b.w.)
Haematology			
RBC (10^6/mm^3)	4.818±0.0422	8.450±0.2668	6.583±0.1956
WBC (mm^3)	6582±16.02	16679±252.0	4953±23.53
Haemoglobin (g/dl)	13.22±0.1515	5.867±0.3007	11.75±0.1784
Platelets(10^3/mm^3)	222.7±1.801	67.33±1.856	179.7±2.155
Biochemical (LFT)			
SGPT (U/ml)	21.48±0.02242	72.20±0.3206	31.59±0.2921
SGOT (U/ml)	27.78±0.1915	58.83±0.8878	28.08±0.1845
ALP (KA units)	10.61±0.01310	27.39±0.01065	12.08±0.08048
Bilirubin (mg/dl)	0.7200±0.01155	3.310±0.03130	0.7683±0.01600
Biochemical (KFT)			
Urea (mg/dl)	21.97±0.04216	46.76±0.05346	60.99±0.3027
Uric acid (mg/dl)	6.702±0.03124	4.462±0.09357	3.752±0.01579
Creatinine (mg/dl)	0.8200±0.01155	0.8233±0.01256	0.7933±0.009545
Glucose (mg/dl)	86.10±0.04913	78.05±0.06167	77.02±0.09542
LPO (nmol/ml)	1.830±0.007303	81.62±0.01740	10.08±0.07351

The data is presented as mean ± SD, n=6, significance at P < 0.05.

Discussion:

Arsenic in the present scenario in South East sub-continent region of Asia has created major health related problems through contamination in underground drinking water. Among possible target organs of heavy metals like arsenic, the kidney and central nervous system appear to be the most sensitive ones. Having been absorbed from the alimentary tract, most of the metals form durable combination with the protein thionein, forming metallothionein, which plays an important role in further metabolism of these metals

[18, 19].The kidney and liver are considered to be the most susceptible organs for metals, because these organs contain most of the metallothionein binding toxic metals [20, 21, 22, 23, 24].These toxic metals also produce free radicals such as lipid peroxides [25]. They encounter with biomembranes and sub-cellular organelles [26,27,28,29, 30,31,32,33,34,35,36].

The abnormally high level of serum SGPT, SGOT, ALP and total bilirubin in the present study are the consequence of arsenic induced liver dysfunction and denotes damage to the hepatic cells. The significant increase in the levels is a direct measure of hepatic injury and they show the status of the liver as there may be cellular leakage and loss of functional integrity of hepatocytes. Furthermore, there was significant increase in the levels of the lipid peroxidation denotes oxidative stress produced by the arsenic leading to high degree of degeneration in the liver cells. But, after administration of *Pterocarpus santalinus* shows significant decrease in the serum LFT levels denotes their hepatoprotective activity. The hepatoprotective effect of *P. santalinus* have been well documented which also proves its antioxidant activity [37]. But, no studies till date have reported any bioremedial study of *P.santalinus* animals against arsenic toxicity. Lipid peroxidation amelioration by *P.santalinus* and its free radical scavenging activity under observation was quite normal but not so effective.

The significant increase in the serum urea, uric acid and creatinine denotes the high degree of degeneration in the nephrocytes. But, administration of *P.santalinus* showed partial amelioration. Thus, this plant *P.santalinus* play a vital role to combat arsenic induced hepatotoxicity and nephrotoxicity normalizing the functions of the two metabolic organs liver and kidney.

Conclusions
In the present times, the study on search for antidote against arsenic induced toxicity is very least shows lacking in this field. The present study is indeed a novel work which deciphers for the first time as the antidote against arsenic induced toxicity. This novel plant *P.santalinus* shows not only hepatoprotective and nephroprotective

activity but also antioxidant activity denotes the elimination of arsenic from the body in *in-vivo* system.

References:

1. Emsley, John (2001). Nature's Building Blocks: An A-Z Guide to the Elements. Oxford: Oxford University Press. pp. 43, 513, 529. ISBN 0-19-850341-5.
2. P.L. Smedley, D.G. Kinniburgh, D.M.J. Macdonald, H.B. Nicolli, A.J. Barros, J.O. Tullio, J.M. Pearce, M.S. Alonso "Arsenic associations in sediments from the loess aquifer of La Pampa, Argentina" Applied Geochemistry 20 (2005) 989–1016.
3. Szinicz L, Forth W. Effect of As2O3 on gluconeogenesis. Arch Toxico 1988; 161:444-449.
4. Singh S, Rana SV. Amelioration of arsenic toxicity by L-Ascorbic acid in laboratory rat. J Environ Biol 2007; 28: 377-384.
5. Shi H, Shi X, Liu KJ. Oxidative mechanism of arsenic toxicity and carcinogenesis. Mol Cell Biochem2004; 255: 67-78.k
6. IARC. Monographs on the Evaluation of the Carcinogenic Risk of Chemicals to Man. Geneva: World Health Organization, International Agency for Research on Cancer, 1972-PRESENT. (Multivolume work). Available at: http://monographs.iarc.fr/index.php p. V84 (2004)]
7. International Legume Database & Information Service: Pterocarpus santalinus FAO Ecocrop: Pterocarpussantalinus, Auroville: Wasteland reclamation through rehabilitation of eroded soil (pdf file)
8. Asian J Androl 2003, 1:27-31. International Legume Database & Information Service: Pterocarpussantalinus, Reitmann S and Frankel S. "A colorimetric method for determination of serum glutamate oxalacetic and glutamic pyruvate transaminases." Amer J Clin Path1957; 28(1): 56-63.
9. Kind, PRN, King, EJ. Estimation of Plasma Phosphatase by Determination of Hydrolysed Phenol with Amino-antipyrine. J Clin Path 1954; 7(4), 322-326.

10. Jendrassik L, Grof P, Vereinfachte. Photometrische Methodenzur Bestimmun des Blubilirubins. BiochemZ 1938; 297, 81-89.

11. Berthelot MPE, Report Chim. Appl, 1859; 2884. Fawcett JK, Scott JE. "A rapid and precise method for the determination of urea". J ClinPathol, 13(2), pp. 1960; 156-159.

12. Bones RW. J BiolChem, pp. 1945; 158-581

13. Bates MN, Smith AH and Hopenhayn-Rich C. Arsenic ingestion and internal cancers- a review. Am J Epidemiol 1992; 135: 462-476.

14. Choudhary H, Harvey T,Thayer WC, Lockwood TF, Stitelor WM, GoodrumPE, Hasset JM and Diamond GL. Urinary cadmium elimination as a biomarker of exposure for evaluating a cadmium dietary exposure – Biokinetics model. J. Toxicol. Environ. Hlth 2001; 63: 221-250

15. Hollis L, Hogstrand C and Wood CM. Tissue specific cadmium accumulation, metallothionein induction and tissue zinc and copper levels during chronic sublethal cadmium exposure in juvenile rainbow t rout. Arch. Environ. Contam. Toxicol, 2001; 41: 468-474.

16. Cui X, Li S, Shraim A, Kobayashi Y, Hayakawa T, Kanno S, Yamamoto M and Hirano S. Subchronic exposure to arsenic through drinking water alters expression of cancer- related genes in rat liver. Toxicologic Pathology2004; 32: 64-72.

17. Kumar A,Ali M, Kumar R, Suman S, Kumar H, Nath A, Singh JK and Kumar D. Withaniasomnifera protects the haematological alterations caused by Sodium Arsenite in Charles Foster rats. International Journal of Research in Ayurveda & Pharmacy (IJRAP) 4 (4), 2013; 491-494.

18. Ramos O, Carrizales L, Yanez L, Mejia J, Batres L, Ortfz D and D faz-Barriga F. Arsenic Increased Lipid Peroxidation in Rat issues by a Mechanism Independent of Glutathione Levels, Environment Health Perspectives1983; 103 (1) : 85-88.

19. Halliwell B and Gutteridge JMC. Free radicals in biology and medicine. 2nd Edition, Oxford University Press (Clrendon) Oxford 1989

20. Rin K, Kawaguchi K, Yamanaka K, Tezuka M, Oku N & Okada S. DNA- strand breaks induced by dimethylarsenic acid, a metabolite of inorganic arsenics, are strongly enhanced by superoxide anion radicals-Biol Pharm Bull,1995; 18 - 45.

21. Yamanaka K, Hoshino M, Okanato M, Sawamura R, Hasegawa A & Okada S. Induction of DNA damage by dimethylarsine, a metabolite of inorganic arsenics, is for the major part likely due to its peroxyl radical, BiochemBiophys ResCommun 1999; 168-58.

22. Marnett L J. Oxyradicals and DNA damage, Carcinogen 2000; 21-361.

23. Basu A, Mahata J, Gupta S &Giri A K. Genetic toxicology of a paradoxical human carcinogen, arsenic - A review, Mutat Res 2001; 488: 171.

24. Valko M, Izakovic M, Mazur M, Rhodes C J &Telser J. Role of oxygen radicals in DNA damage and cancer incidence. Mol Cell Biochem 2004; 266 -37.

25. Kalpana C, Sudheer AR, Rajasekharan KN, Menon VP. Comparative effects of curcumin and its synthetic analogue on tissue lipid peroxidation and antioxidant status during nicotine induced toxicity. Singapore Med J, 2007; 48 (2):124-130.

26. Flora SJS, Bhadauria S, Kannan GM & Singh N. Arsenic induced oxidative stress and role of antioxidant supplementation during chelation - A Review, J Environ Biol 2007; 28 :333

27. Flora SJS, Flora G, Saxena G, Mishra M. Arsenic and Lead Induced Free Radical Generation and Their Reversibility Following Chelation. Cell MolBiol 2007; 53: 24-46.

28. El-Demerdash FM, Yousef MI, Radwan FM. Ameliorating effect of curcumin on sodium arsenite-induced oxidative damage and lipid peroxidation in different rat organs. FoodChemToxicol 2009; 47 (1): 249-254.

29. Manjunatha B.K., Hepatoprotective activity of Pterocarpus santalinus L.f., an endangered medicinal plant. Indian journal of pharmacology, 2006, 38, 25-28.

Chapter-X

Bioremedial effect of Pteris longifolia against of Arsenic induced Toxicity alterations in Charles foster Rats

Pintoo Kumar Niraj*

Abstract

The ubiquitous distribution of arsenic in the environment is being perceived as a matter of global concern. The high prevalence of Arsenic contamination of groundwater in the West Bengal basin, in India is unfolding as one of the worst natural Geo-environmental disaster to date. Chronic exposure of humans to high concentration of arsenic in drinking water is associated with skin lesions, peripheral vascular disease, hypertension, Blackfoot disease and high risk of cancer. Due to which major health related problems are arising in the population. To combat the present problem to the people, a pre-clinical study was done on Charles foster rats. Sodium arsenite alone (8 mg/kg body wt.) per day was administered to these rats for 60 days which caused haematological alterations with significant decrease in Red Blood Cells (RBC's) count, White Blood Cells (WBC's) count, haemoglobin percentage. The biochemical assay shows significant increase in the liver function tests, kidney function tests and lipid peroxidation assay in comparison to control. But, after administration of the novel plant Pteris longaifolia (400 mg/kg body wt.) for 45 days to sodium arsenate pre-treated rats showed significant normalisation in the haematological parameters, biochemical parameters as well as lipid peroxidation levels. The plant not only eliminated the effects of arsenic but also reversed the normal physiological activity in the animal. Thus, thepresent study concludes that novel plant Pteris longifolia possesses the bioremedial impact against Arsenic induced toxicity alterations.

Keywords: Arsenic, Pteris longifolia, Antidote, Amelioration, Preclinical study

---

*Project Assistant, Mahavir Cancer Institute & Research Centre, Patna, Bihar

Introduction

Arsenic contamination has led to drinking water quality degradation across many geographic regions and is now a global socio-economic menace. Arsenic (As) is an environmental and industrial pollutant that affects various organs in human and experimental animals. The major countries affected by arsenic contamination are Argentina, Australia, Bangladesh, Canada, Chile, China, Greece, Hungary, India, Japan, Mexico, Mongolia, New Zealand, South Africa, Philippines, Taiwan, Thailand, USA and USSR [1]. Recently in Bihar, 16 districts have been found to have its ground water contaminated with arsenic in lower Gangetic plains [2]. The arsenic contamination was also observed in three districts Ballia, Varanasi and Gazipur of Uttar Pradesh in the upper and middle Ganga plain, India [3]. Approximately, 20 incidents of groundwater arsenic contamination have been reported from all over the world [4]. Due to groundwater contamination, a large number of populations in India and Bangladesh are suffering from arsenicosis as melanosis, leuco-melanosis, keratosis, hyperkeratosis, dorsum, gangrene, non pettingoedema, skin cancer and skin lesions in sole and palm [5,6,7]. Arsenite in in –vivo condition are transported into cells through aquaglycoporins 7 and 9 which transport water and glycerol. Arsenite binds to cellular sulfhydryl especially the vicinal ones and they interfere with high energy generation [8, 9, 10]. In the tissue, they exert toxic effects through several mechanisms such as reversible combination with sulfhydryl groups. They also inhibit numerous other cellular enzymes such as cellular glucose uptake, gluconeogenesis, fatty acid oxidation and product – ion of glutathione through sulfhydryl group binding[11,12]. The arsenite is also responsible for Reactive Oxygen Species (ROS) generation which leads to cell damage and death through the activation of oxidative sensitive signaling pathways [13]. Since last two decades, the amelioration of various heavy metals borne diseases has gained special attention to researchers. In the present investigation, amelioration against arsenic induced toxicity has been focused on important plant *Pteris longifolia.* *Pteris longifolia* is a fern found in Himalayan sub regions as well as the Gangetic belt of India. It is widely used in the decoration of flower bouquets. However, no studies have reported effect of leaf extract of Pteris longifolia as antidote against arsenic induced toxicity in rats.

Pteris longifolia (commonly known as brake fern) is having the ability to "hyper accumulate" the arsenic from soil. It grows readily in the wild, *Pteris longifolia* is sometimes cultivated. It is grown in gardens for its attractive appearance, or used in pollution control schemes: it is known to be a hyper accumulation or plant of arsenic used in phytoremediation.

Materials and Methods

Animals
Charles Foster rats weighing 160g to 180g of 8 weeks old, were obtained from animal house of Mahavir Cancer Institute and Research Centre, Patna, India (CPCSEA Regd-No. 1129/bc/07/CPCSEA). The research work was approved by the IAEC (Institutional Animal Ethics Committee) with IAEC No. IAEC/2012/12/04. Food and water to rats were provided *ad libitum* (prepared mixed formulated food by the laboratory itself). The experimental animals were housed in conventional polypropylene cages in small groups (2 each). The rats were randomly assigned to control and treatment groups. The temperature in the experimental animal room was maintained at $22\pm2^\theta$ C with 12 h light/dark cycle.

Chemical
Sodium Arsenite (98.5%) manufactured by Biosol Laboratories Pvt. Limited, Kolkata, India was obtained from the Scientific store of Patna.

Preparation of *Pteris longifolia* dose
In the present study, fresh leaves of *P.longifolia* were collected from the local garden of Patna, Bihar. The identity of the leaves of *P.longifolia* was confirmed by Dr. Ramakant Pandey (Botanist), Department of Biochemistry, Patna University, Patna,

Bihar India. The collected leaves of *P. longifolia* were shade dried and were grinded to fine powder. The powder was dissolve in deionised distilled water. The dose was made to 400 mg/kg body weight for oral administration.

Experimental Design

The animals were grouped into 3 groups. Group 1 was Control group (n=6) to which no treatment was given and was designated as healthy control, while to the rest 2 groups (n=18) Sodium arsenite at the dose of 8mg Kg[-1] body weight was administered orally daily for 60 days. Group 2 animals at the end of the Sodium arsenite treatment were dissected for the biochemical assay.

Upon these Sodium arsenite pre-treated groups, *P.longifolia* leaf aqueous extract was administered to Group 3 (n=6) at the dose of 400 mg[-1] Kg body weight orally daily for 45 days. At end of the entire treatment, animals were anaesthetized and dissected and their blood samples were collected and serums were extracted. The serums were then assayed for biochemical study as Liver function tests, Kidney function tests and lipid peroxidation.

Biochemical Evaluation

The Liver Function Test (LFT) as Serum Glutamic Pyruvate Transaminase (SGPT) and Serum Glutamic Oxaloacetate Transaminase (SGOT) were measured according to method [14], Alkaline Phosphate (ALP) by method [15] while total bilirubin activity by method [16]. The Kidney Function Test (KFT) were assayed by methods[17,18] as Urea, Uric acid[19] and Creatinine[20].

Lipid Peroxidation

Thiobarbituric acid reactive substances (TBARS), as a marker for LPO, were determined by the double heating method [21]. The principle of the method was a spectrophotometric measurement of the color produced during the reaction to thiobarbituric acid (TBA) with malondialdehyde (MDA). For this purpose, 2.5 ml of 100 g/l trichloroacetic acid (TCA) solution was added to 0.5 ml serum in a centrifuge tube and incubated for 15 min at 90θC. After cooling in tap water, the mixture was centrifuged at 3000g for 10 min, and 2 ml of the supernatant was added to 1 ml of 6.7g/l TBA solution in a test tube and again incubated for 15 min at 90°C. The solution was then cooled in tap water and its absorbance was measured using Thermo Scientific UV-10 (UV –Vis) spectrophotometer (USA) at 532nm.

Statistical Analysis

Results are presented as mean ± SD and total variation present in a set of data was analysed through one way analysis of variance (ANOVA). Difference among mean values has been analysed by applying Dunnet's t-test. Calculations were performed with the Graph Pad Prism Program (Graph Pad software, Inc., San Diego, U.S.A.). The criterion for statistical significance was set at $P < 0.05$.

Results
Morbidity and Mortality

The rats after the exposure of arsenic (8mg Kg-1body weight per day) for 60 days showed toxicity symptoms such as nausea, nose bleeding, lack of body co-ordination (11 percent of rats showed paralysis like symptoms), blackening of tongue and foot and general body weakness.

Biochemical Changes

The SGPT, SGOT, alkaline phosphatase, total bilirubin, urea, uric acid, creatinine and lipid peroxidation activity showed significant increase ($p < 0.05$) in arsenic treated group in comparison to control rat group. But, these values are significantly lowered ($p < 0.05$) in *P. longifolia* treated group. The biochemical assessment thus shows the hepatoprotective and nephroprotective activity of *P. longifolia* (Table-1).

Blood Parameters	Control (n=6)	Arsenic treated 8mg/kg b.w 60 days (n=12)	*Pteris longifolia* treated 400mg/kg b.w 30 days (n=6)
RBC (10^6/mm^3)	$3.71 \times 10^6 \pm 53083$	$2.51 \times 10^6 \pm 60145$	$4.1 \times 10^6 \pm 33731$
Hb (g/dl)	13.07 ±0.17	6.75 ±0.176	9.9 ±0.5833
WBC (mm^3)	9010 ± 99	7575 ± 241	9958 ± 203
Haematocrit	41.10±5.10	20.25±0.528	28.2±1.518
MCV(fl)	110.78±2.33	161.50±5.02	145.50±3.58
MCHC(g/l)	33.54	33.54	33.54
MCH(pg)	128.3±0.75	154.5±4.23	156.5±2.33
Platelets (mm^3)	187500±6612	73333±3095	179833±3188
Biochemical (LFT)			
SGPT (U/ml)	25.55 ± 1.3501	84.50 ± 1.893	19.92 ± 0.9347
SGOT (U/ml)	27.77 ± 1.307	120.8 ± 1.641	28.00 ± 1.915
ALP (KA units)	8.667 ± 0.6280	29.08 ± 1.519	12.73 ± 0.8743
Bilirubin (mg/dl)	0.4300 ± 0.03307	2.542 ± 0.08796	0.9800 ± 0.03512
Biochemical (KFT)			
Urea (mg/dl)	25.33 ± 0.8819	54.72 ± 1.532	36.75 ± 1.778
Uric acid (mg/dl)	3.483 ± 0.2509	11.72 ± 0.9239	6.938 ± 0.2961
Creatinine (mg/dl)	0.6900 ± 0.03454	1.905 ± 0.05058	0.7733 ± 0.02985
LPO (nmol/ml)	1.802 ± 0.09593	84.13 ± 1.806	7.733 ± 0.4440

Table -1 Changes in the parameters of Charles foster rats exposed to Sodium arsenite at the dose 8 mg/kg body weight daily for 60 days and its bioremedial by *Pterislongifolia* at the dose of 400mg/kg body weight for 45 days.

Discussion

Arsenic in the present scenario in South East sub-continent region of Asia has created major health related problems through contamination in underground drinking water. Among possible target organs of heavy metals like arsenic, the liver, kidney and central nervous system appear to be the most sensitive ones. Having been absorbed from the alimentary tract, most of the metals form durable combination with the protein thionein, forming metallothionein, which plays an important role in further metabolism of these metals [22,23]. The kidney and liver are considered to be the most susceptible organs for metals, because these organs contain most of the metallothionein binding toxic metals [24, 25, 26, 27, 28]. These toxic metals also produce free radicals such as lipid peroxides. They encounter with biomembranes and sub- cellular organelles [29, 30, 31, 32, 33, 34, 35, 36, 37, 38, 39, 40]. The abnormally high levels of serum SGPT, SGOT, ALP and total bilirubin in the present study are the of arsenic induced liver dysfunction and denotes damage to the hepatic cells. The significant increase in the levels is a direct measure of hepatic injury and they show the status of the liver as there may be cellular leakage and loss of functional integrity of hepatocytes. Furthermore, consequence there was significant increase in the levels of the lipid peroxidation denotes oxidative stress produced by the arsenic leading to high degree of degeneration in the liver cells. But, after administration of *P.longifolia* , it shows significant decrease in the serum LFT levels denotes their hepatoprotective activity. The hepatoprotective effect of *P. longifolia* have been well documented which also proves its antioxidant activity. But, no studies till date have reported any bioremedial impact of *P.longifolia* on animals. The arsenic exposure caused immense increase in the serum urea, uric acid and creatinine levels denotes the high degree of degeneration but after administration of *P.longifolia* there was significant decrease in the KFT levels denotes nephroprotective effect.

Conclusion

Thus, *P. longifolia* the novel plants play a vital role to combat arsenic induced hepatotoxicity and nephrotoxicity normalizing the functions of the two metabolic organs liver and kidney. Furthermore, they scavenge the oxidants denotes their antioxidant properties.

References:

[1] Bose R., Mozumdar S. and De A. Hazards of arsenic poisoning, Mini Review ISSN: 2229-6433, 2012, 3(2):23-27

[2] Ghosh NC and Singh RD.Groundwater Arsenic Contamination in India - Vulnerability and Scope for Remedy. Annual Report of Central Ground Water Board (www.cgwb.gov.in/ documents/papers) 2008;1-24.

[3] Ahamed S, Sengupta MK, Mukherjee A, Hossain MA, Das B, Nayak B, Pal A, Mukherjee SC, Pati S, Dutta RN, Chatterjee G,Mukherjee A, Srivastava R and Chakraborti D. Arsenic groundwater contamination and its health effects in the state of Uttar Pradesh (UP) in upper and middle Ganga plain, India- A severe danger. Sci. Total Environ 2006; 370: 310-322

[4] Mukherjee A, Sengupta MK and Hossain MA. Arsenic contamination in groundwater - A global perspective with emphasis on the Asian Scenario. J. Hlth. Popul. Nutri 2006; 24:142-163.

[5] ATSDR Toxicological Profile for Arsenic. Atlanta - Agency for Toxic Substances and Disease Registry 1992.

[6] Karim M. Arsenic in groundwater and health problems in Bangladesh. Wat.Resour, 2000; 34: 304-310

[7] Chauhan S, Flora SJS. Arsenic and Flouride: Two major ground water pollutants. Indian Journal of Experimental Biology 2010; 48: 666-678.

[8] Aposhian, H.V. and Aposhian MM. New development in arsenic toxicity. J.Am. Coll. Toxicol., 1989a; 8, 1297-1305.

[9] Aposhian HV - Biochemical toxicology of arsenic - In Reviews of Biochemistry and Toxicology (Eds: E. Hodgson, J.R. Bend and R.M. Philpot). Vol. 10, Elsevier, New York, 1989b; 265-299.

[10] Aposhian HV, Aposhian MM. Arsenic Toxicology: Five Questions. Chem Res Toxicol; 2006; 19: 1-60.

[11] Szinicz L, Forth W. Effect of As2O3 on gluconeogenesis. Arch Toxico 1988; 161: 444-449.

[12] Singh S, Rana SV.Amelioration of arsenic toxicity by L-Ascorbic acid in laboratory rat. J Environ Biol 2007; 28: 377- 384.

[13] Shi H, Shi X, Liu KJ.Oxidative mechanism of arsenic toxicity and carcinogenesis. Mol Cell Biochem 2004; 255: 67-78.

[14] Reitmann S and Frankel S. "A colorimetric method for determination of serum glutamate oxalacetic and glutamic pyruvate transaminases." Amer J Clin Path 1957; 28 (1): 56-63.

[15] Kind, PRN, King, EJ. Estimation of Plasma Phosphatase by Determination of Hydrolysed Phenol with Amino-antipyrine. J Clin Path 1954; 7(4), 322-326.

[16] Jendrassik L, Grof P, Vereinfachte. Photometrische Methodenzur Bestimmung des Blubilirubins. Biochem Z 1938; 297, 81-89. Berthelot MPE, Report Chim. Appl, 1859; 2884.

[17] Fawcett JK, Scott JE. "A rapid and precise method for the determination of urea". J ClinPathol, 13(2), pp. 1960; 156-159.

[18] Bones RW. J BiolChem, pp. 1945; 158-581, Toro G.& Ackermann PG. Practical Clinical Chem 1975; 154.

[19] Draper HH, Hadley M. Malondialdehyde determination as index of lipid peroxidation. Methods Enzymol 1990; 186:421-31.

[20] Maitani T, N Saito, M Abe, S Uchiyama and Y Saito. Chemical form dependent induction of hepatic zinc-thionein by arsenic administration and effect of co-administered selenium in mice.Toxicol.Lett 1987; 39:63-70

[21] Peraza MA, Fierro FA, Barber DS, Casarez E and Rael LT. Effects of micronutrients on metal toxicity. Environ. Hlth. Perspect 1998; 106: 203-216

[22] Chen C J, Kuo TL and Wu MM. "Arsenic and Cancers.Lancet1. 1988; 414–5. Bates MN, Smith AH and Hopenhayn-Rich C. Arsenic ingestion and internal cancers- a review. Am J Epidemiol 1992; 135: 462-476.

[23] Choudhary H, Harvey T, Thayer WC, Lockwood TF, Stitelor WM, Goodrum PE, Hasset JM and Diamond GL. Urinary cadmium elimination as a biomarker of exposure for evaluating a cadmium dietary exposure – Biokinetics model. J. Toxicol. Environ. Hlth 2001; 63: 221-250

[24] Hollis L, Hogstrand C and Wood CM. Tissue specific cadmium accumulation, metallothionein induction and tissue zinc and copper levels during chronic sublethal cadmium exposure in juvenile rainbow t rout. Arch. Environ. Contam.Toxicol, 2001; 41: 468-474.

[25] Cui X, Li S, Shraim A, Kobayashi Y, Hayakawa T, Kanno S, Yamamoto M and Hirano S. Subchronic exposure to arsenic through drinking water alters expression of cancerrelated genes in rat liver. Toxicologic Pathology 2004; 32: 64-72.

[26] Kumar A, Ali M, Kumar R, Suman S, Kumar H, Nath A, Singh JK and Kumar D. Withania somnifera protects the haematological alterations caused by Sodium Arsenite in Charles Foster rats. International Journal of Research in Ayurveda & Pharmacy (IJRAP) 4 (4), 2013; 491-494.

[27] Ramos O, Carrizales L, Yanez L, Mejia J, Batres L, Ortfz D and D faz-Barriga F. Arsenic Increased Lipid Peroxidation in Rat issues by a Mechanism Independent of Glutathione Levels, Environment Health Perspectives 1983; 103 (1): 85-88.

[28] Halliwell B and Gutteridge JMC. Free radicals in biology and medicine. 2nd Edition, Oxford University Press (Clrendon) Oxford 1989

[32] Rin K, Kawaguchi K, Yamanaka K, Tezuka M, Oku N & Okada S. DNA- strand breaks induced by dimethylarsenic acid, a metabolite of inorganic arsenics, are stronglyenhanced by superoxide anion radicals- Biol Pharm Bull,1995; 18 -45.

[33] Yamanaka K, Hoshino M, Okanato M, Sawamura R, Hasegawa A & Okada S. Induction of DNA damage by dimethylarsine, a metabolite of inorganic arsenics, is for the major part likely due to its peroxyl radical, Biochem Biophys Res Commun 1999; 168-58.

[34] Marnett L J. Oxyradicals and DNA damage, Carcinogen 2000; 21-361.

[35] Basu A, Mahata J, Gupta S & Giri A K. Genetic toxicology of a paradoxical human carcinogen, arsenic - A review, Mutat Res 2001; 488 :171.

[36] Valko M, Izakovic M, Mazur M, Rhodes C J & Telser J. Role of oxygen radicals in DNA damage and cancer incidence. Mol Cell Biochem 2004; 266 -37.

[37] Kalpana C, Sudheer AR, Rajasekharan KN, Menon VP. Comparative effects of curcumin and its synthetic analogue on tissue lipid peroxidation and antioxidant status during nicotine induced toxicity. Singapore Med J 2007; 48 (2):124-130.

[38] Flora SJS, Bhadauria S, Kannan GM & Singh N. Arsenic induced oxidative stress and role of antioxidant supplementation during chelation - A Review, J Environ Biol 2007; 28:333

[39] Flora SJS, Flora G, Saxena G, Mishra M. Arsenic and Lead Induced Free Radical Generation and Their Reversibility Following Chelation. Cell MolBiol 2007; 53: 24-46.

[40] El-Demerdash FM, Yousef MI, Radwan FM. Ameliorating effect of curcumin on sodium arsenite-induced oxidative damage and lipid peroxidation in different rat organs.FoodChemToxicol 2009; 47(1):249-254.

Chapter- XI

Therapeutic Effect of Pteris Longifolia on Hematological Alterations caused by Sodium Arsenite in Charles Foster Rats

Prabhat Shankar*

Abstract

Arsenic is a metal which forms various inorganic and organic compounds. It is classified as metalloids and very dangerous and environmental toxin. Both natural and anthropogenic source are responsible for the distribution of many toxicants mainly heavy metal throughout the environment. It found mainly in rocks in the earth crust as well as nearly in soil, minerals, surface and ground water Twarakavi. Its non metallic form is less reactive but will dissolve when heated with strong oxidizing acids and alkalis.

In this present study, oral administration of sodium arsenite at the dose of 8mg/kg body weight daily caused haematological alterations in rats as manifested by the significant decrease in RBC's count, Haemoglobin percentage, Haematocrit value, Mean cell volume of RBC's (MCV), Mean cell Haemoglobin (MCH), Mean Cell Haemoglobin Concentration (MCHC) and White Blood Cell Count (WBC's). But, after oral administration of ethanolic extract of Pteris longifera at the dose of 500mg/kg body weight daily for 60 days to sodium arsenic pre-treated rats there was an increase in the haematological parameters levels. Thus, the present study shows ameliorative effect of Pteris longifolia against arsenic induced haematological alterations.

Keywords: Pteris longifolia, Sodium Arsenite, Haematological Parameters, Rats

*Ph.D. Scholar, Mahavir Cancer Institute & Research Centre, Patna, Bihar

Introduction

Arsenic is a metalloid which occurs in conjugation with sulphur and metals, and also as a pure elemental crystal (Albertus Magnus). It can exist in various allotropes, although only the gray form has important use in industry. Arsenic appears in three allotropic forms like yellow, black and grey. It tarnishes rapidly in air, and at high temperatures burns forming a white cloud of arsenic trioxide. Arsenic in the atmosphere comes from various sources: volcanoes release about 3000 tonnes per year and microorganisms release volatile methyl arsines to the extent of 20.000 tonnes per year, but human activity is responsible for much more: 80.000 tonnes of arsenic per year are released by the burning of fossil fuels.

Arsenic is found in many countries in the world, in Asia, Bangladesh, China, India, Nepal Taiwan, Vietnam and Myanmar. By" Prior" to the 1970s, Bangladesh had one of the highest infant mortality rates in the world. A little uncombined arsenic occurs naturally as microcrystalline masses, found in Siberia, Germany, France, Italy, Romania and in the USA. China is the chief exporting country, followed by Chile and Mexico. World resources of arsenic in copper and lead ores exceed 10 million tonnes. World health organization (WHO) and US environment protection agency (EPA) had set up the standard for drinking water known as Maximum Contaminant Level (MCL) which is 10 µg/l. Drinking water with MCL or below to MCL is not hazardous to the population. Long-term ingestion of inorganic arsenic other than organic arsenic causes multisystem adverse health effects because organic forms are less toxic and rapidly excreted from body via urine. The clinical manifestations of chronic arsenic exposure are skin lesions, cardiovascular disease, neurological effects, chronic lung disease, cerebro vascular disease, reproductive disease, adverse renal affects, developmental abnormalities, haematological disorders, diabetes mellitus and cancers of skin, lung, liver, kidney and bladder. Low birth weight and adverse pregnancy outcomes are also documented by chronic toxicity of arsenic. Skin manifestation is the early feature of chronic arsenic exposure and cancer is the late phenomenon.

Presence of both melanosis and keratosis are the conformational sign of chronic exposure of arsenic. Arsenic affect the human populations regardless of sex and age but the children are less susceptible to arsenicism ((Frances coni *et al.,* 2002; Wei *et al.* 2007, Concha et al., 1998; Chowdhury et al., 2003).

In India, number of States as - Jharkhand, Bihar, Uttar Pradesh in flood plain of the Ganga River; Assam and Manipur in flood plain of the Brahamaputra and Imphal rivers, and Rajnandgaon village in Chhattisgarh state have chronically been exposed to drinking arsenic contaminated hand tube-wells water above permissible limit of 50 µg/L. Many more North-Eastern Hill States in the flood plains are also suspected to have the possibility of arsenic in groundwater.

In Bihar at least 13 District and 50 Block are affected, but it majorly seen Buxar, Patna, and Bhojpur (Semria Ojhapatti village).Arsenic having a huge toxic effect on human health as well as on animals.Humans may be exposed to arsenic through food, water and air. A very high exposure to inorganic arsenic can cause infertility and miscarriages with women, and it can cause skin disturbances, declined resistance to infections, heart disruptions and brain damage with both men and women. Finally, inorganic arsenic can damage DNA. Organic arsenic can cause neither cancer, nor DNA damage. But exposure to high doses may cause certain effects to human health, such as nerve injury and stomach-aches (Liu *et. al* 2006).

Pteris longifolia (commonly known as brake fern) is having the ability to "hyper accumulate" the arsenic from soil. It grows readily in the wild, *Pteris longifolia* is sometimes cultivated. It is grown in gardens for its attractive appearance, or used in pollution control schemes: it is known to be a hyper accumulate or plant of arsenic used in phytoremediation.

After using *Pteris vittata*, it could be concluded that the other *Pteris* and non-*Pteris* ferns (e.g. *Pteris longifolia, Pteris cretica* and *Pityrogramma calomelanos*) have also been identified to accumulate As. Recently, Kachen ko*et al.,* (2007) found that *P. calomelanos* var. *Austro americana* (Domin) Farw. (Pteridaceae) can accumulate Arsenic in fronds up to 16 415 mg/kg DW in fronds.

Material and Methods

Animals

Charles foster rats (18 female) wt. 150g to 180g of 8weeks old, were obtained from animal house of Mahavir Cancer Institute and Research Centre, Patna, India (CPCSEA Regd-No. 1129/bc/07/CPCSEA). The research work was approved by the IAEC (Institutional Animal Ethics Committee) with IAEC No. IAEC/2012/12/04. Food and water to rats were provided *ad libitum* (prepared mixed formulated food by the laboratory itself). The experimental model were grouped in to two (n=2) and kept in conventional polypropylene cages. The temperature in the experimental animal room was maintained at $22\pm2^{0}C$ with 12 h light/dark cycle. The rats were randomly assigned to control and treatment groups.

Chemical

Sodium Arsenite (98.5%) manufactured by Biosol Laboratories Pvt. Limited, Kolkata, India was obtained from the Scientific store of Patna.

Medicinal plant: Pteris longifolia

The experimental plant *Pteris longifolia* were collected local garden of Patna, Bihar, India. The identify of medicinal plant was confirmed by Dr.Ramakant Panday (Botanist), Department of Biochemistry, Patna University, Patna, Bihar, India. The collected root of *Pteris longifolia* were shade dried and were grinded to fine powder.

Preparation of *Pteris longifolia* dose

In the present study, fresh leaves of *P.longifolia* were collected from the local fauna of Patna, Bihar. The identity of the leaves of *P.longifolia* was confirmed by Dr. Ramakant Pandey (Botanist), Department of Biochemistry, Patna University, Patna, Bihar, India. The collected leaves of *P. longifolia* were shade dried and were grinded to fine powder. The powder was dissolve in deionised distilled water. The dose was made to 400 mg/kg body weight for oral administration.

Experimental Design

The animals were grouped into 3 groups. Group 1 was Control group (n=6) to which no treatment was given and was designated as healthy control, while to the rest 2 groups (n=18) Sodium arsenite at the dose of 8mg Kg-1body weight was administered orally daily for 60 days. Group 2 animals at the end of the Sodium arsenite treatment were dissected for the biochemical assay.

Upon these Sodium arsenite pre-treated groups, *P.longifolia* leaf aqueous extract was administered to Group 3 (n=6) at the dose of 500 mg^{-1} Kg body weight orally daily for 45 days. At end of the entire treatment, animals were anaesthetized and dissected and their blood samples were collected for haematological evaluation.

Haematological Evaluation

The haematological parameters Red Blood Cells Count (RBC's), Haemoglobin percentage (HBG) Haematocrit (HTC) Mean cell volume of RBC's (MCV), Mean cell Haemoglobin concentration (MCHC) and white Blood Cell count (WBC's) were done manually.

Statistical Analysis

The results are presented as mean ± SD and total variation present in a data was analysed through one way. By collecting the calculation report I plot the graph by using the software (Graph pad prism 5.03 Inc., San Diego, USA).

Results

On the basis of experimental results it was observed that the rat after arsenic exposure (8mg/kg/day) for 60 days have shown signs of toxicity such as nose breeding, hair loss, swellings on head was observed (11% of rats showed paralysis like symptoms), blackening of tongue and foot as well as general body weakness .The treated rats shown its gentle recovery.

Haematological changes

Data of haematological parameters are shown in the table, the study shows significant decrease $P<0.0001$ in the Erythrocytes counts (RBCs), Haemoglobin percentage, Haematocrit percentage, MCV,

MCH but significant increases in Leukocyte count (WBC's) in comparison with control group after 60 days of exposure. By using *P. Longifolia*

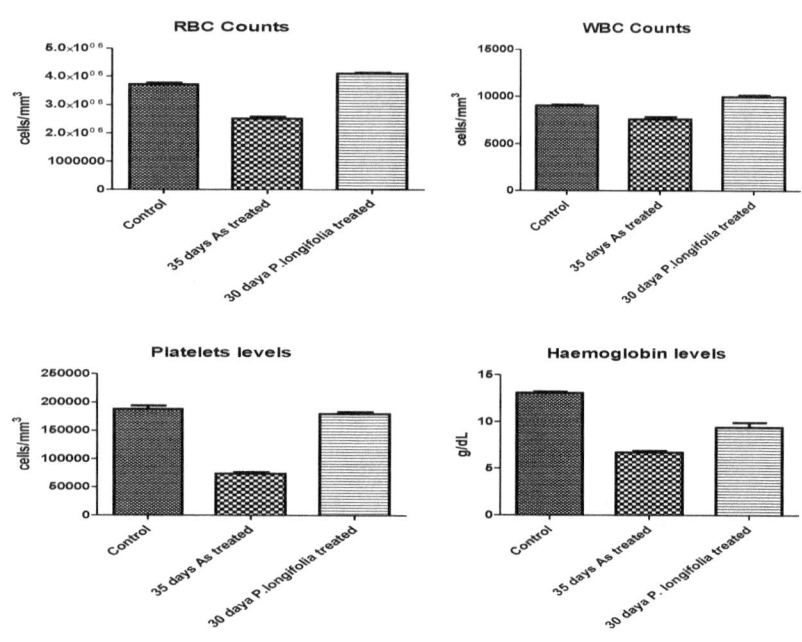

Blood Parameters	Control (n=6)	Arsenic treated 8mg/kgb.w 60 days (n=12)	*Pteris longifolia* treated 500mg/kg b.w 30 days (n=6)
RBC (10^6/mm^3)	$3.71 \times 10^6 \pm 53083$	$2.51 \times 10^6 \pm 60145$	$4.1 \times 10^6 \pm 33731$
Hb (g/dl)	13.07 ±0.17	6.75 ±0.176	9.4 ±0.506
Haematocrit (%)	41.10± 5.10	20.25± 0.528	28.2 ± 1.518
WBC (mm^3)	9010 ± 99	7575 ± 241	9958 ± 203
MCV (fl)	110.78±2.33	161.50±5.02	145.50±3.58
MCHC (g/l)	33.54	33.54	33.54
MCH (pg)	128.3±0.75	154.5±4.23	156.5±2.33
Platelets (mm^3)	187500±6612	73333±3095	179833±3188

Discussion

The arsenic shows diversified toxic effect on human health as well as on animals. Its contamination comes from underground drinking water. The calculated dose of *P.longifolia* gives the better result against Arsenic. This study shows the haematological changes after arsenic exposure as white blood cells (WBCs) label was increased, Red blood cells (RBCs) label were decreased and haemoglobin labels denotes inhibition of hem-synthesis pathway. Arsenic induced cellular toxicity by damaging body's oxidative defence mechanism, *P.longifolia* has potential natural antioxidant and immune modulated property which eliminate the arsenic from the body by chelation therapy (Lee *et al* 2003). It also possesses rejuvenating property by which it maintains the cellular integrity accordingly. Thus, from the entire study it can be concluded that *P.longifolia* ameliorates the haematological alterations in blood by its various properties.

References

1. Chowdhury U. K., Biswas B. K., Chowdhury T. R. (2000). "Groundwater arsenic contamination in Bangladesh and West Bengal, India". Environmental Health Perspectives (Brogan&#3 8) 108:393-397. doi:10.2307/3454378.JSTOR 3454378.
2. Hayes W.J., 2000 — Role of plants, mycorrhizae and phytochelators in heavy metal contaminated land remediation. Chemosphere, 41: 197-207.
3. Khan A.G., Kuek C., Chaudhry T.M., Khoo C.S.,Lasat, MM (2002) Phytoextraction of toxic metals: A review of biological mechanisms. Journal of Environmental Quality 31,109-120
4. Lee DA, Chen A, Schroeder JI (2003) ars1, an Arabidopsis mutant exhibiting increased tolerance to arsenate and increased phosphate uptake. The Plant Journal 35, 637-646
5. Leonard A, Lauwerys R (1980) Carcinogenicity, teratogenicity, and mutagenecity of arsenic. Mutation Research. 75, 49-62
6. Li W, Chen T, Chen Y, Lei M (2005) Role of trichome of Pteris vittata L. in arsenic hyperaccumulation. Science China C Life Sciences 48, 148-154

7. Li Y, Dhankher OP, Carreira L, Balish RS, Meagher RB (2005) Arsenic and mercury tolerance and cadmium sensitivity in Arabidopsis plants expressing bacterial gamma glutamyl cysteine synthetase. Environmental Toxicology and Chemistry 24, 1376-1386

8. Li Y, Dhankher OP, Carreira L, Lee D, Chen A, Schroeder JI, Balish RS, Meagher RB (2004) Overexpression of phytochelatin synthase in Arabidopsis leads to enhanced arsenic tolerance and cadmium hypersensitivity. Plant Cell Physiology 45, 1787-1797

9. Liu Y, Zhu YG, Chen BD, Christie P, Li XL (2005) Influence of the arbuscular mycorrhizal fungus Glomus mosseaeon uptake of arsenate by the As hyperaccumulator fern PterisvittataL. Mycorrhiza 15, 187-192.

10. Liu Z, Styblo M, Rosen BP (2006) Methylarsonous acid transport by aquaglyceroporins. Environmental Health Perspectives.

11. Ma LQ, Komar KM, Tu C, Zhang WH, Cai Y, Kennelley ED (2001) A fern that hyperaccumulates arsenic -A hardy, versatile, fast-growing plant helps to remove arsenic from contaminated soils. Nature 409, 579-579.

12. Mukherjee A., Sengupta M. K., Hossain M. A. (2006). "Arsenic contamination in groundwater: A global perspective with emphasis on the Asian scenario". Journal of Health Population and Nutrition 24: 142–163.

13. Peter Ravenscroft (2007)"Arsenic in drinking water seen as threat, "USAToday.com, "Predicting the global distribution of arsenic pollution in groundwater." Paper presented at: "Arsenic- The Geography of a Global Problem," Royal Geographic Society Arsenic Conference held at: Royal Geographic Society, London, England.

14. Twarakavi, N. K. C., Kaluarachchi, J. J. (2006). "Arsenic in the shallow ground waters of conterminous United States: assessment, health risks, and costs for MCL compliance". Journal of American Water Resources Association 42 (2): 275–294.

Chapter-XII

Antitoxic Evaluation of Foeniculum Vulgare against Sodium Arsenite Induced Nephrotoxicity and Hepatotoxicity in Charles Foster Rats

Chandan Kumar Roy*

Abstract

Arsenic Contamination is present in all around the world. It's an organic compounds classified as metalloids and very dangerous and environmental toxin. It found mainly in rocks in the earth crust as well as nearly in soil, minerals, surface and ground water. Most of the affected countries have made attempts to address this issue; significant gaps remain in the knowledge of the hydrogeological and chemical scope of the problem and the specific health effects of arsenic in Asia. The public health effects of arsenic are a reality and they need to be taken seriously. As the effects of arsenic are long term, it is likely that arsenicrelated disease, with and without fatal outcomes, is going to increase over the coming decades.

Toxicity was induced in Charles Foster rats by Sodium arsenite, administered by Oral Gavage (oral administration) at a dose of 8 mg/kg body weight daily for a period of 36 days. Fennel seeds (dose of 100 mg/kg body weight daily for 30 days) were used as antidote drug against arsenic treated rats. The study shows significant increase in liver and kidney enzymes and LPO levels and decrease in haematological parameters like RBCs, platelets counts and haemoglobin percentage and increase in WBCs in animals treated with sodium arsenite. But, after administration of Fennel there was increase in RBCs counts and decrease in WBCs counts by 5-10% in comparison to controls. Reduced kidney function tests and normalized Lipid peroxidation was observed. Liver function tests showed slight reduction in liver enzymes. Normalized renal tissues and damaged hepatic tissues were observed.

Keywords: Sodium arsenite, organotoxicity, Fennel, Liver function test, Kidney function test, Lipid Peroxidation, oxidative stress

*Research Scholar, Mahavir Cancer Institute & Research Centre, Patna, Bihar

Introduction

Arsenic is one of the most important naturally occurring environmental toxicant and is ubiquitously present in the earth's crust. Millions of people worldwide are suspected to be exposed to arsenic through contaminated drinking water, air and food (Liu et al., 2002).It has mutagenic, teratogenic, and carcinogenic effects (Rossman, 2003). Arsenic is used as herbicide, fungicide, rodenticide and causes air, soil and water pollution.Arsenicals have been accumulated and metabolized in organs like pancreas, liver, kidney, skeletal muscles, adipose tissue and red blood cells (Ademuyiwa and Elsenhans, 2000 ; Paul et al., 2008). Chronic exposure to arsenic has been related to bladder, kidney, liver, skin and lung cancer (Kitchin, 2001).Arsenic exposure has also been associated with severe metabolic disorders such as diabetes, gastrointestinal tract disorders, cardiovascular diseases (Guha Mazumder, 2008), neurological, respiratory, hepatic, hematological, skin, bladder, liver, and lung cancers and reproductive toxicity.Although several hypotheses have been proposed, theexact mechanism of arsenic toxicity has not yet been clearly defined. Several studies suggest that at higher concentrations arsenic exerts its toxicity by generating reactive oxygen species (ROS) during redox cycling and metabolic activation processes that causes tissue damages.Considering arsenic toxicity as one of the serious problems worldwide, its specific, reliable and safe treatment still remained mostly unknown. In recent years, attention is focused worldwide on the potentiality of many dietaryplant products that exert their protective effects against arsenic induced organotoxicity and oxidative stress-mediated diseases by scavenging free radicals.

Foeniculum vulgare (Fennel) commonly known as 'Sauf' in Hindi is a perennial herb belonging to Umbelliferae family. Fennel is widely used as a carminative, both in humans and in veterinary medicine to treat flatulence by encouraging the expulsion of intestinal gas. It contains anethole, which have medicinal effects and is responsible for the carminative action. Its polymers act as phytoestrogens (Dhuley JN 1998). Extracts of fennel seeds have been shown in animal studies to have a potential use in the treatment of Glaucoma.

It also contains another class of bioactive substances called phthalides, which have anticarcinogenic potential. Fennel is used as traditional medicine for its estrogenic, lactogouge, diuretic, analgesic, antioxidant, immune booster and its usefulness in dyspepsia. Fennel seeds contain 1-3% volatile oils, which have disinfectant and anti-inflammatory action, primarily on the respiratory and digestive organs and have an antispasmodic effect on smooth muscle. Antioxidant and antimicrobial activity of fennel has also been reported. Anand *et al.* reported that fennel seed possesses anticancer activity.

Despite the above mentionedbeneficial effect of Fennel seeds, its efficacy in reducing metal toxicity in general and arsenic toxicity in particular, has not yet been studied. Therefore, we aimed to investigate the efficacy of *F. vulgare* on arsenic induced toxicity in rat model. To the best of our knowledge, this is the first study that demonstrates the ameliorative effect of fennel seeds against arsenic toxicity.

Materials and Methods
Experimental Animals
18 Charles Foster rats (Female), weighing 130 gm to 135 gm of 8 weeks old, were obtained from animal house of Mahavir Cancer Sansthan and Research Centre,Patna, India (CPCSEA Regd-No. 1129/bc/07/CPCSEA). The research work was approved by IAEC (Institutional Animal Ethics Committee) of Mahavir Cancer Sansthan. Food and water to rats were provided *ad libitum* (prepared mixed formulated food by the laboratory itself). The experimental animals were housed in conventional polypropylene cages in small groups (3 each). The rats were randomly assigned to control and treatment groups. The temperature in the experimental animal room was maintained at 22 ± 2^0C and relative humidity of $50 \pm 10\%$ with 12 hours light/dark cycle.

Chemicals
Sodium arsenite (98.5%) manufactured by Sigma Aldrich company was obtained from the scientific store of Patna, India. Commercially available kit for Chemical analyses like SGPT, SGOT, Alkaline

Phosphatase, Bilirubin, Urea, Uric acid, and Creatinine was used of crest coral clinical system, Goa, India. Analytical grade TCA, TBA and SDS were purchased from Sigma Aldrich Company.

Collection and Preparation of fennel aqueous extract

In the present study, yellowish green seeds of fennel were purchased from the local market of Phulwarisharif, Patna, Bihar. The identity of the seeds of *F.vulgare* was confirmed by Dr. RamakantPandey (Botanist), Department of Biochemistry, Patna University, Patna, Bihar, India. The collected seeds of *F.vulgare* were shade dried and were grinded to fine powder. The dose was finally made to 100 mg/kg body weight for oral administration by weighing 100 mg of fennel powder and dissolving it in 10 ml of distilled water whenever needed.

Experimental design

All the experiments were done in compliance with theguidelines of Committee for the Purpose of Control and Supervision of Experiments on Animals (CPCSEA). Animals were equally divided into 3groups of 6 rats each and treated sub-chronically as follows-

Group 1: Animals of this group were preserved as normal control

Group 2 and Group 3: Animals of these groups were given by oral gavage the calculated dose of Arsenic as sodium arsenite @ 8 mg/kg body weight once daily for 36 days. The group 2 rats were used as arsenic control. After 36 days of arsenic treatment, the Group 3 rats were given by oral gavage the calculated dose of aqueous extract of *Foeniculum vulgare* @100 mg / kg body weight once daily for 30 days.

After the administration of last dose, these rats were given a one-day rest and kept in fasting overnight and then were sacrificed under light chloroform anesthesia. The hepatic and renal tissues were excised and fixed in 10% formalin for histological studies. Blood was collected by cardiac puncture in EDTA tubes for hematological analysis and serum was separated for biochemical assays like Liver function tests, Kidney function tests and Lipid Peroxidation tests.

Biochemical Analyses

Determination of serum glutamate pyruvate transaminase (SGPT) and serum glutamate oxalate transaminase (SGOT) activity in serum was conducted by Reitman & Frankel's colorimetric method. Activity of alkaline phosphatase (ALP) was determined by Mod. Kind and King's method. Bilirubin activity in serum was estimated by Mod. Jendrassik and Grof's method. Urea level in serum was determined by Mod. Berthelot method. Uric acid activity was determined by Uricase/PAP method while Creatinine activity was determined by Alkaline picrate method. MDA level in blood serum was estimated by Draper and Hadley method (1990).

Haematological Evaluation

The haematological parameters like Red Blood Cell count, White Blood Cell count, Platelets count were done manually whereas estimation of Haemoglobin percentage was carried out by Sahli'scolourmatching method.

Lipid peroxidation (LPO)

LPO refers to the oxidative humiliation of lipids. Thiobarbituric acid reactive substances (TBARS), as a marker for LPO, weredetermined by the double heating method.23 The theory of the method was a spectrophotometric measurement of the colourproduced during the reaction to *thiobarbituric*acid (TBA) with malondialdehyde (MDA). For this intention, 2.5 ml of 100 g/l trichloroacetic acid (TCA) solution was added to 0.5 ml serum in a centrifuge tube and incubated for 15 min at 90^0C. After coolingat room temperature (RT), the mixture was centrifuged at 3000g for 10min, and 2 ml of the supernatant was added to 1 ml of 6.7g/l TBA solution in a test tube and again incubated for 15 min at 90^0C. The solution was then cooled at RT and its absorbance wasmeasured using Thermo Scientific UV-10 (UV –Vis) spectrophotometer (USA) at 532nm.

Histopathological Analysis

Rats were sacrificed from each group for histological analysis. Liver and Kidneys were removed, washed in saline and were fixed in 10 %neutral formalin at roomtemperature for 24 hours. After fixing the tissue, it was thoroughly washed under running water, processed and then embedded in soft paraffin.For each organ serial sections (4-5 μm) were made .These prepared slides were stained with Hematoxylin - Eosin (H & E) and examined morphometrically under LM.

Statistical Analysis

Results are presented as mean ± S.D and total variation present in a set of data was analysed through one-way analysis ofvariance (ANOVA). Difference among means has been analysed by applying Dunnett's't' test at 99.9% (p < 0.05) confidencelevel. Calculations were performed with the Graph Pad Prism Program (Graph Pad Software, Inc., San Diego, USA).

Result

Morbidity and mortality

Rats after Arsenic exposure (8 mg/kg b.w./day) for 36 days have shown signs of toxicity such as sluggishness in the animals especially drowsiness, nausea and giddiness, blackening of tongue and foot. Lack of co- ordination was the prominent observation (some of rats showed paralysis likes symptoms in their limbs). Although, no mortality was observed during exposure of arsenic.

Table 1: Changes in the haematological parameters of Charles foster rats exposed to sodium arsenite @ 8 mg/ kg b. w. daily for 36 days and its amelioration by *Foeniculum vulgare*@ 100 mg/ kg b.w.daily for 30 days.

Blood Parameters	Control (n = 6)	Arsenic treated @8mg/kg b.w. 36 days (n = 12)	*Foeniculumvulgare* treated @ 100mg/kg b.w. 30 days (n = 6)
RBC (10^6/mm^3)	3.66 ± 0.05	2.57 ± 0.11	3.98 ± 0.08
WBC (10^3/mm^3)	7425 ± 234	10333 ± 220	9025 ± 146
Platelets (10^3/mm^3)	186833 ± 6274	73833 ± 2522	180000 ± 3679
Haemoglobin (gm%)	12.95 ± 0.24	6.68 ± 0.21	9.5 ± 0.53

The data are presented as Mean ± S.D., n = 6, Significance at P <
0.0001

Haematological changes

The study showed decrease in haematological parameters like RBCs, platelets counts and haemoglobin percentage and increase in WBCs in animals treated with sodium arsenite. But, after administration of Fennel there was increase in RBCs counts, platelets counts and haemoglobin percentage and decrease in WBCs counts in comparison to arsenic control rats.

Table 2: Antioxidant potential of *Foeniculum vulgare* on lipid peroxidation and ameliorative potential in biochemical related variables in hepatic and renal tissues of sodium arsenite exposed rats.

Biochemical Parameters	Control (n = 6)	Arsenic treated @8mg/kg b.w. 36 days (n = 12)	Foeniculumvulgare treated @ 100mg/ kg b.w. 30 days (n = 6)
SGPT (U/ml)	24.83 ± 0.94	87.92 ± 0.71	75.67 ± 1.52
SGOT (U/ml)	28 ± 1.23	105.8 ± 1.51	94.5 ± 1.65
ALP (KA Units)	5.7 ± 0.19	25.56 ± 0.85	14.97 ± 0.24
Bilirubin (mg/dl)	0.66 ± 0.04	2.45 ± 0.07	1.87 ± 0.07
Urea (mg/dl)	13.92 ±1.16	59.60 ±1.15	21.98 ± 0.72
Uric acid (mg/dl)	6.36 ± 0.19	9.48 ± 0.44	7.14 ± 0.25
Creatinine(mg/dl)	0.89 ± 0.05	2.03 ± 0.06	1.04 ± 0.03
MDA (nmol/ml)	2.26 ± 0.24	53.83 ± 0.82	4.89 ± 0.34

The data are presented as Mean ± S.D.,
n = 6, Significance at P < 0.0001

Biochemical changes

The SGPT, SGOT, Alkaline phosphatase, Bilirubin & Urea, Uric acid and Creatinine activity showed significant increase ($p < 0.0001$) in arsenic treated group in comparison to control rats group. But, these values are significantly lowered ($p < 0.05$) in *F. vulgare* treated group. The biochemical assessment thus shows the hepatoprotective and nephroprotective activity of F.*vulgare* (Table 2). Similarly, MDA activity in the serum of ratsshowed significant increase ($p < 0.0001$) in arsenic treated group in comparison to control rats. But, fennel administration significantly normalized the MDA level (Table 2).and denotes the antioxidant property of Fennel.

Discussion

Arsenic in the present scenario in South East sub- continent region of Asia has created major health related problems through contamination in underground drinking water. Arsenic (As) is a ubiquitous environmental toxicant that induces a broad range of dysfunctions. Among possible target organs of heavy metals like arsenic, the kidney, liver and central nervous system appear to be the most sensitive ones. Most of the metals from durable combination with the protein thionein forms metallothionein and when it is absorbed in alimentary canal, it plays an important role in further metabolism of these metals. Kidneys and liver are considered to be the most susceptible organs for metals, because these organs contain most of the metallothionein that binds toxic metals. In kidneys, arsenic exerts its toxic effects through several mechanisms, the most significant of which is the reversible combination with sulfydryl group of proteins present in the glomerular filtration membrane. It causes oxidative stress by producing reactive oxygen species and nitrogen species which are directly involved in oxidative damage to proteins, lipids, DNA, and ability to interact with thiol group of enzymes as well as proteins which can lead to cellular toxicity and death (Flora et al., 2008).Due to lipophilic nature, arsenic also binds with lipid resulting in decomposition of lipid droplets in the slit pores of glomerular filtration membrane. Both of these reasons are responsible for decreased glomerular filtration rate (GFR), causing retension of nitrogenous waste products into the blood.

The present study has investigated the efficacy of *Foeniculumvulgare* which is considered both a traditional natural medicine and an edible vegetable, against the toxicological disorders induced by sodium arsenite in liver and kidneys using a rat model.The results show that sodium arsenite is potent enough to damage liver, kidney and increase lipid peroxidation as well as to induce changes in the haematological parameters.

In the current study, Arsenic treated group showed a significant increase in serum uric acid, urea and creatinine (Kidney function test) as well as increased serum glutamate pyruvate transaminase (SGPT), serum glutamate oxalate transaminase (SGOT), alkaline phosphatase and bilirubin activity (Liver function test) and MDA levels as compared to normal rats after sub-chronic Arsenic treatment. The study shows haematological changes after arsenic exposure as white blood cells(WBC's) level was increased denotes the necrosis activities in the cells, while decrease in red blood cells (RBC's) and haemoglobin levels denotes inhibition of hem-synthesis pathway. Platelets cells were also significantly reduced (Berberian IG 1989). But, *F. vulgare* treated group showed significant reversal in the biochemical and haematological parameters due to hepatoprotective, nephroprotective and antioxidant properties. The exact mechanism of fennel seed extract is not well known. However, the seed extract could show ameliorating effect dueto presence of essential oils that have antioxidant property.

Antioxidants are substance when present in small quantities prevent the oxidation of cellular organelles by minimizing the damaging effect of reactive oxygen species or oxidative stress.Many reports indicate that there is an inverse relationship between the dietary intake of antioxidant rich foods and incidence of human diseases (Sies, 1993; Halliwell, 1997).

Therefore, on the basis of these results it is suggested that human foods need to be supplemented with fennel seeds to combat the arsenic contaminated water induced organotoxicity.

Conclusion

Thus, from the entire study it can be concluded that aqueous extracts of *Foeniculum vulgare* significantly ameliorates the nephrotoxicity, haematological alterations as well as lipid peroxidation in arsenic induced toxicity in rats by its various properties. It also normalizes the toxicity in liver to some extent. The same dose continued for longer duration might ameliorate the arsenic induced hepatotoxicity at greater extent. It is one of the best antidotes as nephroprotective and antioxidant against arsenic induced toxicity. This is a novel work ever done in the field of toxicology. Further studies are needed to evaluate its pharmacokinetics and toxicity profile to determine its clinical dose and isolation and characterization of bioactive components.

Reference

1. Ademuyiwa, O. and B. Elsenhans (2000): Time course of arsenite- induced copper accumulation in rat kidney. *Biol. Trace Elem. Res.* 74 ,81- 92

2. Arun Kumar, Mohammad Ali, Ranjit Kumar, SwapnilSuman, Hemant Kumar, A. Nath, JK Singh and Dhyanendra Kumar (2013).Withaniasomnifera protects the haematological alterations caused by sodium arsenite in charles foster rats. *Int. J. Res. Ayueveda Pharm. 2013*: 4(4): 491- 494

3. Berberian IG, Enan EE. Hematological studies on white male rats exposed to some antimoulting compounds. *Bull Enviro Contam Toxicol 1989* ; 43 : 60- 65

4. Dhuley JN. Effect of Ashwagandha on lipid peroxidation in stress- induced animals. *J. Ethnopharmacol* 1998 ; 60(2) : 173- 178

5. Draper HH, Hadey M.: Malondialdehyde determination as index of lipid peroxidation. *Methods Enzymol 1990* ; 186: 421- 431

6. Flora, S.J.S., M. Mittal and A. Mehta (2008): Heavy metal induced oxidative stress and its possible reversal by chelation therapy. *Indian J. Med. Res.,*128, 501- 523

7. Guha Mazumdar, D.N.(2008): Chronic arsenic toxicity and human health. *Indian J. Med. Res.* , 128, 436- 447

8. Halliwell, B. (1994a). Free radicals, antioxidants and human disease: curiosity, cause and cosequence?*Lancet; 344:* 721.

9. Jendrassik L and Grof P (1938). Vereinfachte, Photometrische Methodenzur Bestimmung des Blubilirubins; Biochem.; Z(297): 81-89

10. Kind PRN and King EJ (1954). Estimation of Plasma Phosphatase by Determination of Hydrolysed Phenol with Aminoantipyrine; J. Clin. Path.; 7(4): 322-326

11. Kitchin, K.T. (2001): Recent advances in arsenic carcinogenesis: Modes of action, animal model systems and methylated arsenic metabolites. *Toxicol. Appl. Pharmacol.,*172, 249- 261

12. Liu , J., B. Zheng, H.V. Aposhian , Y. Zhou , M.L. Chen , A. Zhang and M.P. Waalkes : Chronic arsenic poisoning from burning high arsenic containing coal in Guizhou , China. Environ. Hlth. Pers., 110 , 199- 222 (2002)

13. Paul ,D.S. ,V. Devesa , A. Hernandez – Zavala , B.M. Adair , F.S. Walton , Z. Drobna , D.J. Thomas and M. Styblo : Environmental arsenic as a disruptor of insulin signaling. *Met. Ions Biol. Med.*, 10 , 1- 7 (2008)

14. Reitmann S and Frankel S (1957). A colorimetric method for determination of serum glutamate, oxalate and glutamic pyruvate transaminases; Amer. J. Clin. Path.; 28 (1): 56-63

15. Rossman, T.G. (2003) Mechanism of arsenic carcinogenesis: an integrated approach. *Mutation Research-Fundamental and Molecular Mechanisms of Mutagenesis*, 533(1-2), 37–65.

Chapter- XIII

Water birds of Loktak Lake at Ramsar site in North East India: Conservation Issues

Oinam Sunanda Devi*

Abstract

Loktak Lake is the first Ramsar site of north-eastern India which is threatened from continuous human pressure from the last two decades resulting loss of biodiversity. Data on bid species abundance were collected using distance sampling methods. A total of 6162 individuals from 65 species of water birds belonging to 13 families were encountered at undisturbed (UD), moderately disturbed (MD) and disturbed (D) habitats of the Lake including two globally threatened species. Of the total water birds encountered, 22 are Omnivorous, 40 Picivorous and 3 were Insectivorous in their feeding guilds. Out of 65 water bird species, 31 are winter migrants, 2 are passage migrants and 32 are resident species. I used moderately disturbed and disturbed habitat to compare with undisturbed habitat Loktak Lake to examine the effects of disturbance on avifaunal assemblages of Loktak Lake ecosystem. It was found that undisturbed habitat of the Lake support higher diversity of birds than disturbed and moderately disturbed habitats and also they support more threatened and restricted range species. The findings will help in formulating future conservation programs of the Lake and its biodiversity as a whole.

Key Words: Conservation, Disturbance, Loktak Lake, Threatened water birds, Wetland

---

*Post-doc Fellow, Manipur University, Imphal

Introduction

The State of Manipur falls in the Indo- Burma global biodiversity hotspot (1), (2) and the Eastern Himalaya Endemic Bird Area (3). Situated on the far eastern corner of India bordering Myanmar, Manipur has nine Important Bird Areas (4). The Loktak Lake is the first Ramsar Site of North east India and an important IBA which provides refuge to thousands of birds. But due to intense hunting pressure and general disturbances, the waterfowl number of the Lake has declined in recent years (5). There are reports of birds such as the White Stork- Ciconia ciconia, Greater Adjutant Stork- Leptoptilos dubius, Spot-billed Pelican- Pelecanus phillipiensis and Greater Spotted Eagle- Aquila clanga from the Lake during 1980s (6). There are also old reports of occurrence of Eastern Sarus Crane, Grus Antigone on the Lake (7). Besides hunting and poaching of water birds, loss of vegetation cover in the catchment area and the construction of Ithai barrage on the Lake also account for rapid decline of waterfowl number (8).

It is suggested that birds are convenient indicators of general biodiversity of a region (9), and are also useful in monitoring environmental changes (10). Endemic and threatened birds with restricted ranges are more vulnerable to habitat destruction than any other birds. As the disturbance continues, ecosystem inputs and outputs are altered threatening previously existing core habitats resulting in a progressive erosion of biological diversity (11); (12).

Considering the above facts, the present study was conducted to provide information on the current avifaunal assemblages of the Lake and also to see the effects of small scale habitat disturbance on the diversity and distribution of water birds.

Study Area

The Loktak Lake is the largest freshwater lake of north-eastern which is also the first Ramsar site of the region. The lake forms an important bird area of Manipur, IBA Site No. IN-MN- 06. It lies in the geographical area of 24^0 34' 60" N latitudes and 93^0 49' 60" E longitudes and its altitude varies between 767- 813 msl. The Lake has a maximum length of 26 km and width of 13 km and is about 2.7

m deep (4). There are 14 hills on the southern part of the Lake, varying in size and elevation, appearing as islands. Prominent among them is Sendra, Ihing and Thanga islands (4). The whole Loktak wetland system also comprises small wetlands such as Phumlen (3,500 ha), Ikop (2,600 ha), Waithou (257 ha) and Lousi (450 ha) pats. The Keibul –Lamjao National Park which is home to the highly endangered Manipur Brow-antlered Deer Cervus eldi eldi forms the southern portion of the lake. It is the only floating National park formed by large continuous mass of swamp with floating mats of vegetation, locally known as phumdis, covering much of its surface. The vegetation comprises of Zizania latifolia, Leersia hexandra, Phragmites karka, Cepithipedium spp., Carex spp., Saccharum munja, Narenga porphyrochroma and Polygonum perfoliatum (4).

On the basis of human disturbance, the wetland habitat was categorized into three types: i) disturbed (D) habitat comprising the Lake periphery where there is maximum human activity, ii) moderately disturbed (MD) habitat which consists of open waters and floating mats vegetation where fishing activities occur, and iii) undisturbed (UD) habitat which consists of undisturbed open waters in the middle of the Lake with few floating vegetation mats where no or minimum fishing activity occurs.

Method

Field surveys were conducted for a period of two years from April 2010 up to March 2012, 8 days on average each month (total 192 field days). The surveys followed fixed-width line transect method (13). Altogether 12 randomly selected transects of 3 km length and 50m breadth were laid, 4 transects each on the three major habitats types i.e. Undisturbed (UD), Moderately Disturbed (MD) and Disturbed (D) habitats. Opportunistic observations were also considered for the list so as not to miss any species during the survey period. Feeding guilds were classified as per direct observations and available literature. (14). The identification of bird species and knowledge of their geographic ranges are based on the information of available books. (14), (15).

The geographic distribution range was categorized on a scale of 1-5 (smaller to largest): (1) eastern Himalayas Yunan and Northern

Indo-china, (2) Northeastern India and all Indochina, (3) Indo-Malayan region, (4) Indo- Australian region or Australasia tropics, (5) Palaeotropic and above (16).

The common and scientific names of the birds given in the checklist followed the IOC list (17). The threatened status of the birds given in the checklist is as per IUCN Red List of Threatened Species (18), (19), and (20). The abundance and movement patterns of birds were largely based on available literature (21). Data were analyzed using the statistical software Species Diversity and Richness version 3.0. Diversity was estimated in terms of species richness and evenness, as well as using the Shannon-Wiener index, which combines richness and abundance into a single measure (22) and bootstrap method was used to calculate 95% confidence intervals for Shannon-Wiener's indices. In order to test for differences in diversity between habitats, pair-wise randomization tests were carried out based on 10,000 re-samples of species abundance data (23). Percentage cumulative abundance was plotted (K dominance) against log species rank (24) for comparing diversity between samples. The species richness was estimated using rarefaction (25).

The transact data of three habitat studied (relatively undisturbed (UD), moderately disturbed (MD) and disturbed (D) habitats) were computed to evaluate proportional to undisturbed habitats, by the use of the following formula: ut/ut + mdt + dt, where ut= total bird census data of habitat 'UD'; mdt = total bird census data of habitat 'MD'; and dt = total bird census data of habitat 'D'. The Propund data were arcsine transformed for analysis. The transformed data were filtered if it fulfilled the condition of ut + mdt + dt > = 5 and only selected data were used for analysis. The independent variable ranked species distribution was compared with arcsine transformed data of species abundance in different habitat categories through analysis of variance (ANOVA). Pearson's correlation coefficient was also computed to test the significance between the variables. Only significant results were presented.

Results

Species Assemblages

A total of 6162 individuals of 65 species of water birds belonging to 13 avian families were encountered in the survey. Of them, 22 species are omnivorous, 40 picivorous and 3 were insectivorous in their feeding habits. With regard to migratory status, 31 species are winter migrants, 2 passage migrants and 32 are residents. Of the total migratory species 15 are common and 16 are rare while among the residents, 21 are common and 11 are rare. Two globally threatened species are also included among the total species recorded namely Oriental Darter Anhinga melanogaster (NT) and Ferruginous Pochard Aythya Nyroca (NT). Some notable migratory rare species includes Northern Shoveler Anas clypeata, Red-crested Pochard Rhodonessa rufina, Common Pochard Aythya ferina, Tufted Duck Aythya fuligula, Graylag Goose Anser anser, Bar-headed Goose Anser indicus, Great Crested Grebe Podiceps cristatus, Gadwall Anas strepera, Spot-billed Duck Anas poecilorhyncha, Mallard Anas platyrhynchos, Pallas's Gull Larus icnthyaetus and Brown-headed Gull Larus brunnicephalus etc. (Appendix I).

Monthly Diversity Variations

The monthly Shannon-Wiener diversity indices analysis of water birds shows that the indices ranged between 2.024 and 3.865 (Table 1). Comparison of monthly diversity between samples (transact data) shows that, the diversity indices were higher during the month of January, December, February, November and was lowest in the month May followed by April and September respectively at 5% level (TABLE 1; Fig. 2).

The analysis of diversity ordering (using right tailed sum methods) in different monthly samples show that, the diversity was different in each month's sample in which the highest diversity was found in the month of January and December (Fig. 3).

Table Showing Total monthly species diversity indices of avifauna of Loktak Lake during the study period

Months	Shannon Weiner Index (H)	Variance H	Lower 95%	Upper 95%
APR	2.295	0.003365	2.156	2.382
MAY	2.024	0.006776	1.798	2.127
JUN	2.57	0.00505	2.369	2.647
JUL	2.498	0.005275	2.272	2.562
AUG	2.111	0.008539	1.809	2.182
SEPT	2.345	0.004834	2.127	2.398
OCT	2.776	0.001381	2.671	2.814
NOV	3.497	0.0007295	3.409	3.514
DEC	3.698	0.0006334	3.626	3.726
JAN	3.865	0.0004307	3.805	3.885
FEB	3.64	0.0007919	3.556	3.665
MAR	2.996	0.001166	2.902	3.036

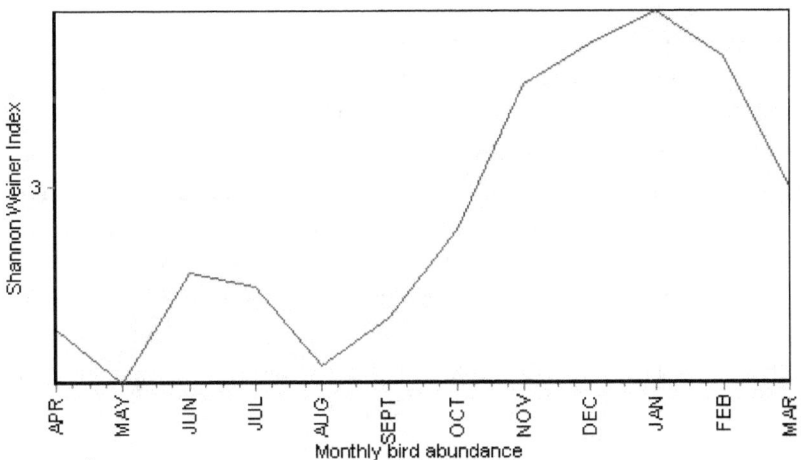

Figure Showing Plot of Shannon Weiner Indices of monthly bird abundance data of Loktak Lake during the study period

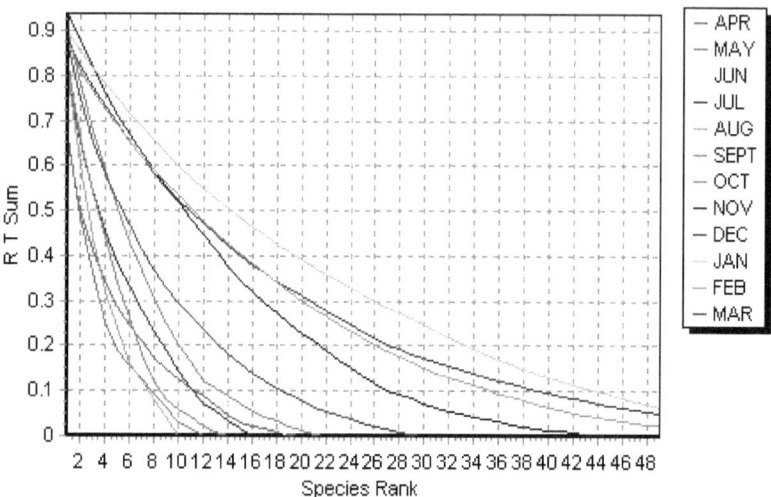

Figure Showing Month-wise Diversity Ordering in Right Tailed Sum against Species Rank of abundance

Species Diversity at different habitat Categories

Highest number of species are recorded at Undisturbed (n = 51), compared with Moderately Disturbed (n = 44) and Disturbed (n = 37) habitats (TABLE 2). The Shannon- Weiner estimate of diversity was significantly higher at the undisturbed habitat than the disturbed habitat at 5% level (TABLE 2; UD vs. D randomization test, Δ = - 0.53, P = 0.01), again it was also higher in moderately disturbed habitat compared to that in the disturbed habitat (TABLE 2; MD vs. D randomization test, Δ = 0.41, P= 0.01). But, it appeared similar when moderately disturbed and undisturbed habitats were compared (Table 2; UD vs. MD randomization test, Δ = 0.11, P= 0.0003; Table: 2).

Similarly, the percentage cumulative abundance plotted (K dominance, Fig. 4) against log species rank for comparing diversity between samples (UD, MD & D) showed that "UD" (lower line) has higher diversity than "D" habitat but in undisturbed habitat (UD) and moderately disturbed habitat (MD), K dominance line cross each other and thus shows to rank differently for different diversity indices.

Simpson and Shannon means followed by the same letter are not significantly different at the 5% level (pair wise randomized test based on 10,000 random samples). Rarefaction test was done for species richness based on present absent data of each transact of the habitat UD, MD &D.

Table Showing Species richness, abundance and diversity of water

	Habitat category		
	UD	MD	D
Individuals	2391	1949	1822
Species (total = 65)	51	44	37
Richness (SE)	51 (0.2)	44 (0.22)	37 (0.02)
Simpson	35.1 (± 4.64)	34.18 (± 5.12)	19.95 (± 3.64)
Shannon-Weiner(H) (Variance)	3.75 (0.0003538)	3.63 (0.0003511)	3.22 (0.0007254)

Abbreviation: UD = Undisturbed; MD = Moderately Disturbed; D = Disturbed.

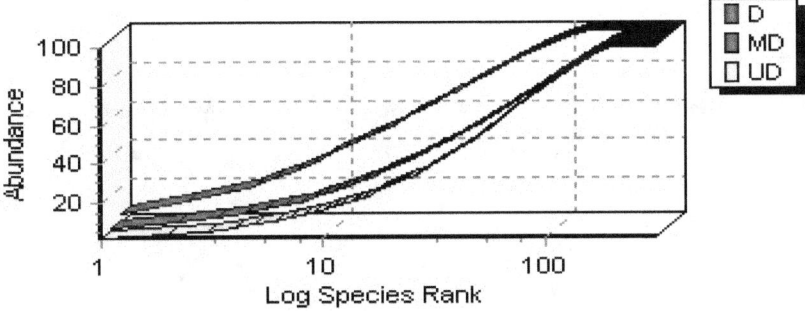

Figure 4. K dominance plotted for comparing diversity among UD, MD & D habitat samples. UD line goes lower which indicate the higher diversity than the other two.

Effects of habitat disturbances on geographical distribution of water birds

Birds species sampled at undisturbed habitat (UD) had more restricted geographical distribution than those sampled at disturbed (D) and moderately disturbed (MD) habitats (ANOVA; $F_{4,65}$ = 13.07, P<0.0005; Fig 5; TABLE 3). There was a significant relationship between undisturbed habitat preferences of water birds and their geographical distribution ranges.

The species with narrow geographic distribution ranges tend to confine at undisturbed habitat, whereas species with wider geographical ranges were more often found at the disturbed habitat (Fig 5). The univariate analysis of variance also showed significant results with comparison between species geographic ranges and feeding guild (arcsine transformed data as dependent variable; ANOVA performed results was, $F_{4,65}$ = 11.87; P<0.027).

Table Showing Results of ANOVA performed with dependent variable Arcpund with two other independent variables, food and geographical range of distribution and their interaction.

Source	SS	d f.	MS	F	P
Intercept	14.856	1	14.856	81.682	.000***
Food	4.093	2	2.046	5.320	.007**
Range	2.223	4	2.64	13.07	.000*
Food*Range‡	10.756	4	2.689	11.866	.027*
Error	10.56	65	.174		
Total	82.424	69	2.15		

ns= not significant; *** = highly significant; * significant; ‡= comparison between two factors; R^2 = .585; adjusted R^2 = .377

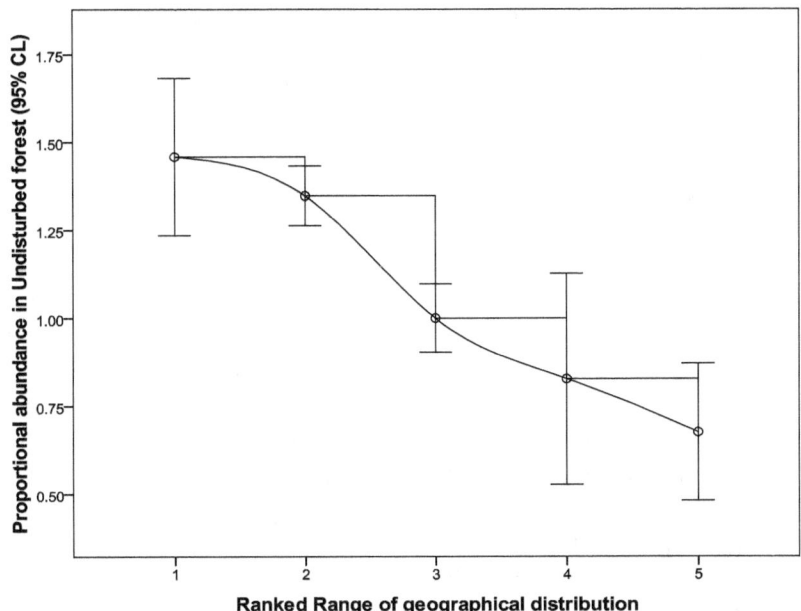

Figure Showing Relationship between proportional abundance at Undisturbed habitat with ranked species geographical distribution range (ANOVA, P<0.0005)

Conclusion

The Loktak Lake is the largest natural freshwater lake in northeast India playing an important role in the ecological and economic security of the region ([4]). The Lake provides refuge to a large number of water fowls of more than 21 species earlier but their number is gradually declining recently due to intense hunting pressure and general disturbance ([5]). Present study records a total of 65 water bird species including 17 Anatids at the three categories of habitats studied. Of the total, 51 species were encountered within undisturbed habitat, whereas, 37 species were recorded from disturbed habitat and 44 species are confined to moderately disturbed habitat. It was observed that large number of waterfowl species were congregated within the undisturbed and moderately disturbed habitat site, where there is no or minimum disturbance from the fishing communities. Globally Near-Threatened species such Anhinga melanogaster and Aythya nyroca were found mostly at undisturbed habitat. The study also reveals that water bird diversity was highest during the winter season than the summer and monsoon season, apparently from the fact that large number of migratory water fowl species visits the lake for feeding and nesting during the winter season.

It was further noted that the number of threatened water fowls recorded were less compare to earlier studies (4), (5), (7). Species such as Spot-billed Pelican Palecanus philippensis and Greater spotted Eagle Aquila clanga were not recorded during the study period. Rapid habitat deterioration was accounted for the decrease in waterfowl numbers of the lake. But large congregation of species such as Lesser-whistling Teal Dendrocygna javanica, Garganey Anas querquedula, Common Teal Anas creca etc were encountered during the study which still helps the Lake in retaining the Ramsar site status.

The ongoing habitat disturbances such as total removal of phumdis (vegetation mats), intense hunting of water birds and overfishing by local people leads to scarcity of food and cover for the water birds. Apart from hunting and other general disturbances, the one of the main reason for the decrease of waterfowl number in the Lake is the construction of Ithai barrage for a multipurpose hydro electric and irrigation project. The blocking of the Khordak channel (outlet of the lake water towards Chindwin-Irrawady river system) more or less alters the Lake ecosystem by converting the fluctuating water level into a reservoir with more or less constant water level thereby bringing about basic hydrological changes (4). The Dam also affects the abundance of migratory fish species such as Cirrhina reba (locally called as Ngaton) and Osteobrama belangeri (locally called a Pengba) (Singh, 1989). The Ithai Barrage effectively blocked the migratory route leading to a virtual demise of these traditional fisheries. Likewise the numbers of other migratory fishes were also declined leading to gradual decline in fish population of the Lake which also affects the water fowl population.

Therefore, in order to save the declining water birds and the lake ecosystem as a whole, conservation awareness programs among the local people are required immediately. The programs must be planned in a continuous process to sensitize the people about the importance of the water birds and sustainable use of the wetland resources to conserve it for future generations. Conservation measures must be adopted in such a way that local people must be involved in the activities and also some alternative livelihood means must be provided to the phumdi dwelling fisher folks otherwise they will continue to exploit the Lake and its produce. We must also understand the plight of the local people for whom the Lake and its resources are their only means of survival. Therefore, the present conservation scenarios of the Lake are among the complicated ones and require thorough measures to protect both the Lake and its biota without compromising the livelihood of the local people.

References:

[1] N. Myers, R. Mittermeier, C. Mittermeier, G. da Fonseca and J. Kent Biodiversity hotspots for conservation priorities, Nature, 2000, 403: 853–858.
[2] R. A. Mittermeier, P. R. Gill, M. Hoffmann, J. Pilgrim, T. Brooks, C. G. Mittermeier, J. Lamoreux and G. A. B. da Fonseca, Hotspots Revisited: Earth's Biologically Richest and Most Endangered Terrestrial Eco regions (Cemex Books on Nature, USA. 2004, 497pp).
[3] A.J. Stattersfield, M.J. Crosby, M. J. Long and D. C. Wege, Endemic Bird Areas of The World: Priorities for Biodiversity Conservation (Birdlife International. Cambridge, U.K. Conservation Series 7, 1998, 846pp).
[4] M. J. Islam and A.R. Rahmani, Important Bird Areas in India: Priorities Sites for Conservation. (Indian Bird Conservation Network: Bombay Natural History Society and Birdlife International, UK, 2004, 1133pp).
[5] T, H. Singh and R. K. S. Singh, Ramsar Sites of India: Loktak Lake (World Wide Fund for Nature, New Delhi, 1994, 69pp).
[6] L.Sanjit, D. Bhatt and R. K. Sharma, Habitat heterogeneity of the Loktak Lake, Manipur. Current Science, 2005. 88 (7): 45- 45.
[7] J. C. Higgins, The game birds and animals of the Manipur State with notes on their numbers, migration and habitats. Journal Bombay Natural History Society, 1934, 37: 81-95.

[8] T. Manihar, Loktak (Newsletter of Loktak Development Authority and Wetland International, South Asia, 1999, 1:1-5).

[9] ICBP, Putting Biodiversity on the Map (Bird life International, Cambridge, UK, 1992).

[10] R.W. Furness, J. J. D Greenwood and P. J. Jarvis, Can birds be used to monitor the Extinction debt. Nature, 1993. 371: 65-66.

[11] J. Terborgh and B. Winter, Some causes of extinction. In: Soule, M. E., Wilcox, B. A. (Eds.), Conservation Biology: An evolutionary Ecological perspective. Sinauer Associates, Sunderland, MA, 1980, 119-133.

[12] D. Tilmans, R. M. May, C. L. Lehman and M. A, Nowak Habitat destruction and the extinction debt. Nature, 1994, 371: 65-66.

[13] C.J. Bibby, N.D. Burgess and D.A. Hall, Bird Census Techniques (Academic press, London, New York, San Deigo, Boston, 1992, 248pp).

[14] S. Ali and S.D. Ripley, A Compact Handbook of the Birds of India and Pakistan (Second Edition. Oxford University Press, 1987, 737pp).

[15] R. Grimmet, C. Inskipp and T. Inskipp, The Pocket Guide to the Birds of Indian Subcontinent (Oxford University Press, 2000, 888pp).

[16] B. F. King and E. C. Dickension, Birds of South East Asia (Herper Collins Publisher, London, 1975 480pp).

[17] F. Gill and M. Wright, Birds of World: Recommended English Names (Princeton NJ: Princeton University Press, Version 2.2, 2006, generated on 2009-08-25).

[18] Bird Life International, Threatened Birds of Asia: The Bird Life International Red Data Book—Vol. 1 (Birdlife International, Cambridge, UK, 2001a, 1516pp).

[19] Bird Life International, Threatened Birds of Asia: The Bird Life International Red Data Book—Vol. 2. (Birdlife International, Cambridge, UK, 2001b, 1517–3038pp).

[20] IUCN, IUCN Red List Categories and Criteria: Version 3.1 (Second edition, Gland, Switzerland and Cambridge, UK: IUCN. Available at www.iucnredlist.org/ technical-documents/categoriesand-criteria, 2012b).

[21] P.K. Saikia and M.K. Saikia, Diversity of Bird Fauna in N.E. India, Journal of Assam Science Society, 2000, 41(2): 379–396.

[22] E. Magurran, Ecological Diversity and its measurement (Chapman and Hall, 1988, 192pp).

[23] R. Solow, A simple test for change in community structure, Journal of Animal Ecology, 1993, 62(1):191-193.

[24] P. J. D. Lambshead, H. Platt and M. Shaw, Detection of differences among assemblages of marine benthic species based on an assessment of dominance and diversity. Journal of Natural History, 1983, 17: 859-874.

[25] K. L. Heck, G. V. Belle and D. Simberloff, Explicit calculation of the rarefaction Diversity measurement and the determination of sufficient sample size. Ecology, 1975, 56: 1459- 1461.

APPENDIX-I: Checklist of Water birds of Loktak Lake during the study period.

Sr. No	Family	Common Name	Scientific Name	Status	F. Guild	G R*
1	Anatidae	Ruddy Shelduck	Tadorna ferruginea	WM, C	P	3
2		Common Shelduck	Tadorna tadorna	WM, C	P	3
3		Lesser-whistling Duck	Dendrocygna javanica	R, C	P	3
4		Fulvous-whistling Duck	Dendrocygna bicolor	WM, r	P	3
5		Gadwall	Anas strepera	WM, r	P	3
6		Spot-billed Duck	Anas poecilorhyncha	WM, r	P	3
7		Mallard	Anas platyrhynchos	WM, r	P	3
8		Garganey	Anas querquedula	WM, C	P	3
9		Northern Pintail	Anas acuta	WM, C	P	3
10		Common Teal	Anas creca	WM, C	P	3
11		Northern Shoveler	Anas clypeata	WM, r	P	3
12		Red-crested Pochard	Netta rufina	WM, r	P	3

13		Common Pochard	Aythya farina	WM, r	P	3
14		Ferruginous Pochard	Aythya nyroca	NT, WM, C	P	3
15		Tufted Duck	Aythya fuligula	WM, r	P	3
16		Greylag Goose	Anser anser	WM, r	P	3
17		Bar-headed Goose	Anser indicus	WM, r	P	3
18	Ciconidae	Open-bill Stork	Anastomus oscitans	R, C	P	3
19	Ardeidae	Cattle Egret	Bulbulcus ibis	R, C	O	3
20		Little Egret	Egretta garzetta	R, C	P	3
21		Large Egret	Casmerodius albus	R, C	P	3
22		Little Heron	Butorides striatus	R, C	P	3
23		Indian Pond Heron	Ardeola grayii	R, C	P	3
24		Purple Heron	Ardea purpurea	R, r	O	3
25		Black-crowned Night Heron	Nycticorax nycticorax	R, C	P	3
26		Cinnamon Bittern	Ixobrychus cinnamomeus	R, r	P	3
27		Yellow Bittern	Ixobrychus sinensis	R, r	P	3
28	Podicipitidae	Little Grebe	Tachybaptus ruficollis	WM, r	P	3
29		Great Crested Grebe	Podiceps cristatus	WM, r	P	3
30	Phalacrocoracidae	Indian Cormorant	Phalacrocorax fuscicollis	R, r	P	3
31		Great Cormorant	Phalacrocorax carbo	WM, C	P	3
32		Little Cormorant	Microcarbo niger	R, C	P	3
33	Anhingidae	Oriental Darter	Anhinga melanogaster	NT, R, r	P	3
34	Rallidae	White-breasted	Amaurornis	R, C	O	3

			Waterhen	phoenicurus			
35		Watercock	Gallicrex cinerea	R, r	O	3
36		Purple Swamphen	Porphyrio porphyrio	R, C	O	3
37		Common Moorhen	Gallinula chloropus	R, C	O	3
38		Common Coot	Fulica atra	R, C	O	3
39	Jacanidae	Bronzed-winged Jacana	Metopidius indicus	R, C	O	3
40		Pheasant-tailed Jacana	Hydrophasianus chirurgus	R, r	O	3
41	Charadriidae	Little Ringed Plover	Charadrius dubius	R, C	O	3
42		Lesser Sand Plover	Charadrius mongolus	WM, C	O	3
43		Little Stint	Calidris minuta	WM, C	O	3
44		Temminck's Stint	Calidris temminckii	WM, C	O	3
45		Red-wattled Lapwing	Vanellus indicus	R, C	O	3
46		River Lapwing	Vanellus duvaucelii	NT (2012) R, r	O	2
47		Northern Lapwing	Vanellus vanellus	WM, r	O	1
48	Scolopacidae	Common Snipe	Gallinago gallinago	WM, r	O	3
49		Pintail Snipe	Gallinago stenura	WM, C	O	3
50		Common Greenshank	Tringa nebularia	WM, C	O	3
51		Common Sandpiper	Actitis hypoleucos	WM, C	O	3
52		Marsh Sandpiper	Tringa stagnatilis	WM, r	O	3
53	Laridae	River Tern	Sterna aurantia	R, C	O	3
54		Pallas's Gull	Larus ichthyaetus	PM, r	P	3
55		Brown-headed Gull	Larus brunnicephalu	PM, r	P	3

s

56	Alcedini dae	White-breasted Kingfisher	Halycyon smyrensis	R, C	P	3
57		Common Kingfisher	Alcedo atthis	R, C	P	3
58		Crested Kingfisher	Magaceryle lugubris	R, C	P	1
59		Ruddy Kingfisher	Halycyon coromanda	R, r	P	2
60		Oriental Dwarf Kingfisher	Ceyx erithacus	R, r	P	3
61		Pied Kingfisher	Ceryle rudis	R, C	P	3
62		Blue-eared Kingfisher	Alcedo meninting	R, r	P	3
63	Motacilli dae	White Wagtail	Motacilla alba	WM, C	I	5
64		Grey Wagtail	Motacilla cinerea	WM, r	I	5
65		Citrine wagtail	Motacilla citreola	WM, C	I	5

Abbreviation: R- Resident, C- Common, r- Rare; WM- Winter Migrant, PM, Passage Migrant; NT- Near Threatened; P- Picivorous, C- Carnivorous, O- Omnivorous, I- Insectivorous.

*Geographical Range (GR):
The geographic distribution range was categorized on a scale of 1-5 (smaller to largest): (1) eastern Himalayas Yunan and Northern Indo-china, (2) Northeastern India and all Indochina, (3) Indo-Malayan region, (4) Indo- Australian region or Australasia tropics, (5) Palaeotropic and above.

Chapter-XIV

Efficacy of Some Bangladeshi Botanical Extracts for Controlling of Pests in Brinjal Field

Md. Abul Kalam Azad*

Abstract

Bangladesh is rich in floral biodiversity. It supports approximately 5000 species of angiosperms. The efficacy of nine Bangladeshi botanical extracts was tested for controlling of pests in experimental brinjal field of Rajshahi University. Accordingly, water extracts of dried leaves of Nicotiana tabacum, Aegle marmelos, Allium satiuum, Ficus hispida, Lawsonia inermis, Viter negundo and seeds of Carum roxburghian, Corchorus capsularis and Swietenia macrophylla were prepared and sprayed on experimental brinjal plot. Out of these nine botanicals, Nicotiana tabacum leaves extract showed best performance against the selected pest attack compare to other extracts. Ficus hispida leaf extract also showed good activity in the protection of brinjal plant from pest. The efficacy of Aegle marmelos and Ficus hispid leaf extracts was found same in brinjal plot against the pest attack. However, Carum roxburghianum extract showed lowest efficacy, hampered the normal plant growth of brinjal and reduced the yield of brinjal fruits compare to other botanicals.

Keywords: Botanicals, biodiversity, extract, activity, pest

*Associate Professor, Institute of Environmental Science, Rajshahi University, Rajshahi, Bangladesh

Introduction

Brinjal/Eggapple (Solanum melongena L), belongs to the family Solanace, is one of the most popular and nutritious vegetables worldwide. Adaptability to wide range of soil and climate is the main reason for its world wide extensive cultivation. China is the first in cultivating and consuming eggplant. It is a cheap source of carbohydrate and vitamins. In a subtropical country like Bangladesh, eggplant is grown all over the country on medium high land to high land in both Rabi and Kharif seasons. It is positioned the 2nd in acreage, production, yield and in consumption next to potato. In the year 2006-2007, total 360,000 acres land were under eggplant cultivation, total production was 399,000 mt and yield was 2.52 mt/acre. Eggplant is attacked by a number of pests, insect, nematodes and disease causing fungi during various stages. At least fifteen insect pests and one mite pest are found to attack the eggplant/eggapple. Among them, eggplant shoot and fruit borers, stem borer, leaf sucker, leafhoppers and epilachna beetles cause serious damage to the crop [1]. One of the major factors of low yield of eggplant is pest attack. The brinjal leaf sucker (pest) has been found to be a serious pest of brinjal in Bangladesh. Both the nymphs and adults of the hopper cause serious damage to the leaves by sucking the cell sap. The small nymphs suck sap from the lower surface of the leaves. The entire plant turns brown and show burn symptom and ultimately the leaves droop off.

The use of conventional insecticides has raised some concern about their threat to the environment and development of insecticide resistance in insects [2], there is an imperative need for the development of safer, alternative crop protectants such as botanical insecticides. Current pest control technology is based largely on imported synthetic insecticides, which are frequently priced beyond easy reach of small holder, farmers, who constitute a very large proportion of the farming population in Bangladesh.

Moreover, many insects been reported to be resistance to chemical insecticides like malathion, DDT, Lindane, Demitan methyl, Pyrethroidestc [3][4]. The problem caused by pesticides and their residues have increased the need for effective, biodegradable pesticides with greater selectivity. Alternative strategies have included the search for new types of insecticides and the re-evaluation and use of traditional botanical pest control agents [5]. Bangladesh and many other Asian countries are rich in plant products and traditionally used by the rural inhabitants for medicinal purpose and in some instance as preparations for insect control [6]. Botanical insecticides tend to have broad spectrum activity, are relatively specific in their mode of action, and easy to process and use in farm-levels. They are also safe for higher animals and the environment [7]. Botanical insecticides can often be easily produced by farmers and small-scale industries, indigenous plant materials are cheaper and hazard free in comparison to chemical insecticides [8]. Plants are rich sources of natural substances that can be utilized in the developemnt of environmentally safe methods for insect control [9]. Crude plant extracts often consist of complex mixtures of active compounds, they many show greater overall bioactivity compared to the individual constituents [10] [11]. The deleterious effects of crude plant extracts on insects were manifested in several ways, including toxicity [12] and feeding inhibition [13][14]. Certain plant families, particularly Meliaceae, Rutaceae, Asteraceae, Labiateae, Piperaceae and Annonaceae were viewed as exceptionally promising sources of plant-based insecticides [15][16][17].

The research in botanical pesticides has a good scope of study. Bangladesh is rich in plant biodiversity. Therefore, it may be possible to find out the suitable combinations and formulations of different indigenous botanicals to produce an eco-friendly plant based pesticide for sustainable pest management in Bangladesh. This study was carried out to verify the botanical pesticidal activity of nine plants materials in e-experimental brinjal field of Rajshahi University.

Materials and Methods

The field experiment was conducted in experimental research field of Rajshahi University. The experiments were performed during March 2012 to June 2012. The land of the experimental plot was ploughed with power tiller and was pulverized by 4 times ploughing followed by laddering. The weeds and stubbles were removed from the field. The soil was properly leveled for planting. After opening the land, well decomposed cowdung was applied and thoroughly mixed up with soil. Before final land preparation, inorganic fertilizers were applied. Fertilizer and manure dose were calculated on the basis of fertilizer Recommendation Guide of BARC. Several holes were made every 50 cm interval and line to line 1 meter. About 35-40 days old brinjal seedling (local variety kanta) were purchased from bazar and planted in each hole. Watering and other intercultural operations were done as and when necessary.

Design of Experimental Plot

The plot was arranged CRD with three replications. Nine botanical treatments and one control (tap water) were applied in this experiment).

Preparation of Botanicals for Spray

Plant leaves of Ficus hispida, Aegle marmelos, Nicotiana tabacum, Lawsonia inermis, Vitex negundo, bulb of Allium sativium, Seeds of Swietenia macrophylla, Carum roxburghian, Corchorus capsularis and Swietenia macrophylla were collected from Rajshahi City. Before grinding or cutting, the plant parts were dried up in lab for 20-25 days. About 100 gm of leaf dusts or grinding seeds were dissolved in one litre of tap water in a plastic bucket and kept for three days and were filtered through cheese cloth and preserved in refrigerator until use.

Spray and Monitoring

The botanical solution was sprayed on brinjal experimental plot twice a week with the help of a sprayer. The pest was monitored every day and damages were counted every 3- days in a week. The numbers of infested leaves were also recorded. All data were analyzed by ANOVA and means separated using Duncun's multiple range tests (p=0.05).

Results and Discussion

In present study, effect of nine plant extracts was tested in experimental brinjal field. Out of these, Nicotiana tabacum leaves extract (3.63±0.96) showed excellent performance against the pests like leaf roller, whitefly and jassid in brinjal field compare to control (8.80±0.50). Ficus hispida leaf extracts was also showed good performance (6.80±0.34) against the pests attack (Tables 1 & 2).

The activities of Vitex negundo, Carum roxburghian, Corchorus capsularis and Swietenia macrophylla extracts were nearly same to control treatment, whereas Allium sativum and Lawsonia inermis extract enhanced the pest attack (Tables 1 & 2). Aegle marmelos leaf extracts showed moderate protection against the pests. All the results mentioned above are highly significant ($p<0.05$). These results are in agreement with the findings of [18]. They noted that the extracts from neem, cinnamon (Cinnamomum cassia), anise (Illicium verum) and fennel (Foeniculum vulgare) as well as cinnamon oil, horseradish oil and mustard oil acted rapidly against pest and caused over 80% mortality to eggplant shoot and fruit borer.

Plant extract was found to have profound effect on the physiology of plants. Nicotiana tabacum leaves extracts showed maximum plant height (42.33±2.40 cm) in comparison to control treatment (26.66±3.38 cm). Ficus hispida leaves extract treatment showed second highest growth of brinjal plant, 31.00±4.04 cm (Table 3). Carum roxburghian and Swietenia macrophylla seed extracts showed relatively lower plant growth (16.33±2.18 and 15.33±2.96 cm, respectively) than Nicotiana tabacum and Ficus hispida. Carum roxburghian and Swietenia macrophylla seed extracts were found to phytotoxic to brinjal plants and showed negative plant growth compare to control (Table 3). Out of nine plant extracts, Nicotiana tabacum leaves extract showed highest brinjal production (421.28±208.05g) compare to control (80.25±41.81g). Besides the Ficus hispida treatment, other seven treatments individually produced lowest level of brinjal compare to control treatment (Table 3).

Table Showing Effect of plant extracts against pest attack on brinjal leaves

Name of Treatments	Number of infected leaves
Mehidi (Lawsonia inermis)	9.03 ±.95ab
Nishinda (Vitex negundo)	8.40 ±.75abc
Tobacco (Nicotiana tabacum)	3.63 ±.96d
Garlic (Allium sativum)	9.26± .46a
Soj (Carum roxburghianum)	7.46 ±.78abc
Bell (Aegle marmelos)	6.96 ±.29bc
Khoksha (Ficus hispida)	6.80 ±.34c
Jute (Corchorus capsularis)	8.56± .32abc
Mahagoni (Swietenia macrophylla)	7.90 ±.20abc
Control	8.80 ±.50abc

Values in a column having same letter did not differ significantly (P=0.05) by DMRT

Table Showing Pest observed in Brinjal Field

Name of Treatment	Pest Observed
Mehidi (Lawsonia inermis)	Jassid, leaf hopper, leaf roller, white fly and red ant
Nishinda (Vitex negundo)	Jassid, leaf hopper, shoot borer and red mite
Tobacco (Nicotiana tabacum	Jassid and whitefly
Garlic (Allium sativum)	Red mite, whitefly, jassid, beetle and leaf hopper
Soj (Carum roxburghianum)	Leaf roller, red mite, whitefly, jassid and beetle
Bell (Aegle marmelos)	Jassid, leaf hopper and leaf roller
Khoksha (Ficus hispida)	Red ants, jassid and leaf hopper
Jute (Corchorus capsularis	Red ants, jassid, beetle, whitefly
Mahagoni (Swietenia macrophylla	Red ants, jassid and leaf hopper
Control	Red ants, leaf roller, jassid, leaf hopper, shoot borer and whitefly

Table Showing Effect of plant extracts on plant height and brinjal production

Treatments	Plant height (cm)	Production (g)
Mehidi (Lawsonia inermis)	25.00±2.08bcde	30.67± 5.81b
Nishinda (Vitex negundo)	22.33± 1.45cdef	50.80± 11.72b
Tobacco (Nicotiana tabacum)	42.33± 2.40a	421.28± 208.05a
Garlic (Allium sativum)	18.66 ±1.33def	.00± .00b
Soj (Carum roxburghianum)	16.33 ±2.18f	.00 ±.00b
Bell (Aegle marmelos)	26.00± 1.52bcd	91.87± 58.30b
Khoksha (Ficus hispida)	31.00± 4.04b	68.05 ±41.90b
Jute (Corchorus capsularis)	17.66 ±1.20ef	55.71± 42.57b
Mahagoni (Swietenia macrophylla)	15.33 ±2.96f	42.52 ±24.57b
Control	26.66± 3.38bc	80.25± 41.81b

Values in a column having same letter did not differ significantly (P=0.05) by DMRT

Nicotiana tabacum leaves extract showed potent activity to enhance leaves production (40.33±14.26) compare to control (13.00±6.11). As like as Nicotiana tabacum the extract of leaves of khoksa (Ficus hispida) was also found to enhance the brinjal plant to produce more leaves (27.66±8.11) (Table-4).

Table Showing Effect of plant extracts on brinjal leaves

Treatments	Total number of leaves	Leaves containing days	Numbers of spray
Mehidi (Lawsonia inermis)	16.66± 3.28ab	42.66±1.45f	10
Nishinda (Vitex negundo)	12.66 ±6.17b	42.33±1.45f	10
Tobacco (Nicotiana tabacum)	40.33 ±14.26ab	122.33± 1.45a	20
Garlic (Allium sativum)	10.33± 2.60b	52.33± 1.45e	11
Soj (Carum roxburghianum)	8.33± 3.33b	42.66 ± 1.45f	10
Bell (Aegle marmelos)	21.33± 9.20ab	52.33 ±1.45e	10
Khoksha (Ficus hispida)	27.66 ±8.11ab	60.00 ±2.88d	11
Jute (Corchorus capsularis)	23.00± 10.69ab	87.66 ±1.45b	14
Mahagoni (Swietenia macrophylla)	25.33± 5.81ab	70.00 ±2.88c	19
Control	13.00± 6.11b	41.00 ±2.08f	15

Nicotiana tabacum treatment was found to contain leaves for long term period (122.33±1.45 days) compare to control (41.00±2.08). Where as in other eight treatments brinjal plant was found to leave leaves within a short period of time (Table 4).

During this study, we observed that both the nymphs and adults of the hopper cause serious damage to the leaves by sucking the cell sap. Eventually the entire plant turned brown and showed burn symptom and ultimately leaves droop happened. Leaves containing days are high in both Nicotiana tabacum (122.33±1.45) and Corchorus capsularis (87.66±1.45) compare to control (41.00±2.08).

The main compounds of plant extracts are mono-terpenoids. These botanical compounds offer promising alternatives to chemical insecticides. These compounds may act as effective insecticides against vegetables pests [19], [20], contact insecticides [21], [22], repellents [23] and antifeedants [24].

Conclusion

Out of nine plant extracts, tobacco (Nicotiana tabacum) laves extract showed excellent performance against all kinds of hoppers (jassid, whitefly and leaf roller), on the contrary garlic bulb (Allium sativum) extract showed very poor efficiency to protect the brinjal plant from pest attack. Mahagoni (Swietenia macrophylla) and soj (Carum roxburghianum) seeds extract was found to hamper the plant growth of brinjal. Alternatively, Nicotiana tabacum enhanced the brinjal plant growth as well as production and increased the duration of life cycle of plant.

References:

[1] BARI, Annual Report 1993-94, Bangladesh Agricultural Research Institute, Joydebpur, Gazipur, Bangladesh. –BBS, 1995, 103.
[2] H. S. Huang, N. T. Hu, Y. E. Yao, C. Y. Wu, S. W. Chiang and C. N. Sun, Molecular cloning and heterologous expression of a glutathione S- translcrasc involved in insecticide resistance from the diamond back moth, Plutella xylostella. Insect Biochemistry and Molecular Biology, 28, 1998, 65 1-658.
[3] B.R. Champ and J. W. Crihb, Lindane resistance in Sitophilusoiy:ac> (I,) and Silophilus zeamais Molsch. (Coleoptera, curulionidae) in Queensland, Journal of Stored Products Research. 1, 1985, 9-24.
[4] W. R Halliday, F. H. Arthur and F. H. Zettler, Resistance status of red flour beetle (Coleoptera: Tenebrionidae) Infesting stored peanuts in south eastern United States, Journal of Econmic Entomology, 81, 1988, 74-77.
[5] J. V. D. Heyde, R. C. Saxena and H. Schmutterer, Neem oil and neem extract as potential insecticides for control

of hemipterous rice pest, Proc. 2nd International Neem conf., Rauischholzhausen, 1984, 377-390.

[6] F. A. Talukder and O.E. Howse, Deterrent and insecticidal effects of extract of pithraj, Aphanamixis polistachya against Tribilium castanium in Storage, Journal Chemical Ecology. 19 (11), 1993, 2463-2471.

[7] Annonymous, Recommendations of the symposium on resources for sustainable agriculture; The use of neem and other plant materials for pest control and rural development, neem symposium. XVII Pacific Science Cngress (Honolulu; East-west center), 1991, 1-11.

[8] R. C. Saxena, N. J. Liqudo and H. B. Justo, Neem seed oil an antifecdanl for brown plant hopper. Proc. 1st. Int. Neem Conf. Rottach, Egern, W. Germany, June, 1980, 171-188.

[9] M. M. Sadek, Antifeedant and toxic activity of Adhaloda vasicq leaf extract against Spodopleru littoralis (Lepidoptera: Noctuidae), Journal Applied Entomology, 27, 2003, 396-404.

[10] M. R. Berenbaum, J. K.. Niato and A. R. Zangerl, Adaptive variation in the furanocoumarin composition of Pastinaca saliva (Apiaceae), Journal Chemical Ecology, 17, 1991, 207-215.

[11] W. Chen, M. B. Isman and S. F. Chiu, Antifeedant and growth inhibitory effects of the limonoid toosendanin and Mclia loosendan extracts on the variegated cutworm, Peridroma saucia, Journal Applied Entomology, 119, 1995, 367-370.

[12] I. G. Hiremath, J. A. Young, I. Kim-Soon and S. Kim, Insecticidal activity of Indian plant extracts against Nilaparvata lugens (I lomoptcra: Delphacidae), Applied Entomology and Zoology, 32, 1997, 159-166.

[13] K. D. Klepzig, and F. Schlyter, "Laboratory evaluation of plant derived antifeedants against European pine weevil, Hylobius abietis" Journal of Economic Entomology, 92, 1999, 644-650.

[14] D. A. Wheeler and M.B. Isman, Antifeedant and toxic activity of Trichilia Americana extract the larvae of Spodoptera litura, Entomologia Experimentalis et Applicata, 98, 2001, 9-16.

[15] M. Jacobson, Botanical insecticides. Past, present and future. In: Insecticides of Plant Origin. American Chemical Society (Amazon, J. T., Philogene, B. 1. R.and Morand, P. eds.), Symposium Series No. 387, Washington, D.C., 1989, 1-10.

[16] I. I. Schmutterer, Properties and potential of natural pesticides from the neem tree, Annual Review of Entomology, 30, 1990, 698-700.

[17] M. B. Isman, Leads and prospects for the development of new botanical insecticides. In: Reviews in Pesticide Toxicology (Roe, R. M. and Kuhr, R. J. eds.), Vol. 3. Toxicology Communications Inc., Raleigh, NC, 1995, 1-20.

[18] A. Cork, S.N. Alam, N.S. Talekar and R.C. Jhala, Development and commercialization of mass trapping for control of eggplant borer in South Asia. Proceeding of 4th International Conference on Biopesticides: Phytochemicals and natural products for the progress of mankind'. 13-18 February 2005, Chiang Mai, Thailand.

[19] A. Cork, M.J. Lies, N.Q. Kamal, J.C.S. Choudhury, M.M. Rahman and M. Islam, An old pest, a new solution - Commercializing rice stem-borer pheromones in Bangladesh, Outlook on Agriculture, 34(3), 2005, 181-187.

[20] H. Muyinza, P. C. Stevenson, H. Talwana, D. R Hall, D. I. Farman and R. O. Mwanga, Root Chemicals could offer opportunities for breeding for Sweet Potato Resistance to the Weevil Cylas puncticollis Boheman (Coleoptera: Apionidac). Aspects of African Biodiversity: Royal Society Of Chemistry Special Publication, 321, 2010, 49-57.

[21] H. K.. Kim, J. R. Kim and Y. J. Aim, Acaricidal activity of cinnamaldehyde and its congeners against Tyrophagus putrescentiae (Acari: Acaridae). Journal of Stored Products Research. 40, 2004, 55-63.

[22] A. L. Tapondjou, C. Adler, D. A. Fontem, H. Bouda and C. Rcichmuth, Bioactivitics of cymol and essential oils of Cupressus sempervircns and Eucalyptus saligna against Sitophilus zeamais Motschulsky and Tribolium confusum du Vai, Journal of Stored Products Research, 41(1), 2005, 91-102.

Chapter-XV

Shirui Kashong Biodiversity Conservation and Sustainable Development

Ninghorla Zimik T.*

Abstract

Biodiversity may be defined as the sum total of species richness i.e. the numbers of species of plants, animals and microorganism occurring in a given region, country, continent or the entire globe. Shirui Kashong is situated in the extreme Indo-Myanmar border of Ukhrul district in Manipur which is included in the 25th biodiversity hotspots of the World. The mountain with its unique eco-system is the home of many endemic rare flora and fauna. There are more than 150 herbaceous flowering plants and through out the year different kinds of flowers bloom profusely in succession. The mountain is also a home to rare animals and birds like Black Panther, Tragopan, Shirui Tiger, Hume Barbacked etc. However due to climate change and excessive deforestation for economic purposes, many rare species have started disappearing. The rich biodiversity should be conserved through in situ and ex situ conservation. The villagers who are solely dependent on forest resources should be given an alternative means of livelihood by conserving biological diversity which constitute an essential aspect of sustainable development.

Keywords: *Biodiversity, Conservation, Shirui Kashong, Shirui Lily, Sustainability*

*Associate Professor, Pettigrew College Ukhrul, Manipur

Introduction

Shirui Kashong Mountain is situated in the extreme corner Indo-Myanmar border of Ukhrul district of Manipur in North East India. North East India, being at the confluence of three major bio-geographical realm of the World is extremely rich in flora and fauna of the diversity. With more than 225 tribal indigenous communities, the North East is a treasure house of biological and cultural identity. The tropical climate of the regions with high rainfall and plenty of sunlight coupled with unique bio-geographical positioning of this region is responsible for rich biodiversity in terms of floral and faunal elements [1]. Manipur state of North East is included in the two biodiversity hotspot of the World i.e. Eastern Himalayan and Indo-Myanmar which ranks 6th among the 25th biodiversity hotspots of the world. The state is rich in both biological and cultural diversity. Out of the 16 Forest types in the country, this small state Manipur has 6 types. "More than 60% of the geographical area off the state is under forest" [2]. Being situated in the Biodiversity Hotspots, the state has, many endemic species, not found anywhere else in the World. A biodiversity hotspots is a region with a high level of endemic species that is under threat. Ukhrul district of Manipur state where Shirui Kashong is located is 83 kms away from the state capital Imphal.

The present Ukhrul district covers an area of 4544 sq.kms bounded by Myanmar in the East, Nagaland state in the north, Senapati and Imphal district in the west and Thoubal and Chandel District in the south. The traditional boundaries however got fragmented to different districts of Manipur and Myanmar. The "Tangkhul habitat spread beyond the Indian border in upper Burma in Somra tract and Naga hills of Burma" [3]. Ukhrul district is unexplored hidden place which is a home to rare flora and fauna. "The scenic beauty of the country, the productivity of its soil, the healthy and bracing climate of the region has been testified by many who have visited this part of the country" [4]. The beauty of Shirui Kashong manifests the grandeur of God's creation. It is also described as a "Hidden Paradise, a Shangrila beckoning to be explored" [5]. It is a border district stretching about 200 kms of International boundary, Ukhrul district offers a great scope for border trade and would serves as gateway of India to South East Asia and China.

The district is inhabited by the Tangkhul Nagas who belong to Mangolian racial group and speak Tibeto-Burman language. However, "the ethnologist and anthropologists agree that the Nagas have been formed by a mingling of peoples...chinese-Tai blood, Tibeto-Burman and the Aborigines of present Assam state" [6]. The Tangkhul Nagas are believed to have migrated from Huang Ho and Yangze rivers which lies in the Zinziang province of China. "Oral history of Tangkhul Hao people said that they were living in the Zingzing valley in China and reached the present land" [7]. Many Scholars including European scholars observed that among the Tangkhuls, they found people like classic Aryans. "The Tangkhuls have sharp features like Aryans with slight Mongoloid touch having complexion with pure Aryan group, e.g. Iranians, Afgans or Kashmiris" [8]. From the above facts, we can guess that during ancient days, a pure Aryans wave might have passed through Tangkhuls belt causing a new tribe bringing about a mixture of Aryans and Mongoloid [9]. W. Ibohal Singh also wrote that the tribe to which Gautama Buddha belonged used to perforate the ears like that of the Tangkhul culture.

The Tangkhuls have rich culture and tradition which are in the form of songs, legends, myth, folklore etc. They strictly observed gennas and taboos. Their beautiful arts and craft speak volumes of their heritage which stands the test of time and reflects the culture and lives of the people. The mystic blue mountain ranges, hills and dales adorn with lustful green forests spotted with varied hue of seasonal flowers throughout the seasons vibrates and echoes with the sound of music, songs, dances, festivals and agriculture activities harmonizing with the tune of nature makes the land vibrant and lively. From the beginning of the year till December, they are engaged in the various field works and festivals. Naga festivals and songs are mostly agriculture oriented. Celebration of different festivals is a part and parcel of the Naga lives capital to Shirui kashong is 98 kms. It is situated at about 15 kms east of the district headquarter Ukhrul. Shirui Kashong is best known to the World for its only begotten endemic ground lily called Lilium Macklinae (Shirui Lily) and for its rich biodiversity. The mountain is strikingly beautiful and it is paradise unexplored where varities of flowers bloom in succession through out the year round. Shirui Lily is declared as state flower since 21-03-1989. The altitude of the Peak is 1715m – 2553m above the sea level. The average temperature of the mountain is 2.8°C to 33°C with occasional snowfall having subtropical hill and mid temperate climate with wet summer and cold winter. Nearly the whole of Shriui Kashong and its adjoining hill range Phangrei Peaks are composed of Chromites containing partly metallurgical grade and serpentine rocks. Shirui Kashong has three divisible portions of hills namely Shongrei (highest and biggest) Shongrah (lower and smaller hill) and Sarumkatong Peak where wild animals occasionally appear for play or recreation. The garden point which is located at an altitude of about 2986 metres above MSL is endowed with salubrious climate. Seven rivers originated from Shrui Kashong mountain namely Singuira Kong (Kong mans river) Namra Kong, Kokti kong, Maret kong, Yangui kong, Rajik Kong and Nga Yai sari kong. It is said that the number of rivers coincide with the number of lily flower colours. Out of the seven rivers, Shinguira and Maret rivers made to their courses towards Ukhrul and Kokti and Razik rivers merged with the Chindwin rivers in neighbouring Myanmar.

According to popular legends of the Tangkhul, Shirui Kashong is the abode and flower garden of goddess Shirui Philava or Princess. It is popularly narrated that Shirui Princess is exceedingly beautiful and used to appear donning in white flowing like sari looking for spotless handsome young man. It is said that she is now married and is not seen anymore.

"Tangkhul people look upon this mountain with respect, fear and wonders...British Administrators and anthropologists regards the mountain as the centre of distribution of Tangkhul people over the length and breadth of the hill. William Pettigrew had a great look at all the hill ranges from the top of Shirui Kashong before starting his missionary work in 1896"[10]. In the olden days, Shirui Kashong was like Noah's ark for the Tangkhuls for its rich and unique biodiversity

Objectives
1. To conserve the rich biodiversity of Shirui Kashong in situ and ex situ conservation.
2. To establish Life Science Research Institute.
3. To bring sustainable Development.

According to U.N. convention on Biological Diversity 1992 –Article 2– Biodiversity or biological diversity means the variability among living organism from all sources including inter-alia, terrestrial, marine and other aquatic ecosystem and the ecological complexes of which species, between species and of ecosystem. The term biodiversity was coined by Walter and Rosen in 1985 which was formed by a contraction of the word biological diversity. Biodiversity has become a familiar term only after the United Nations Conference on the Environment and Development (UNCED) which was held at Rio-de-Janeiro (Brazil) in 1992. The conference laid immense stress on the biological diversity of our earth planet and the need to preserve it for posterity. Biodiversity has been defined in common parlance as "the sum total of species richness i.e. the number of species of Plants, animals and microorganism occurring in a given region, country, continent or the entire globe"[11]. The term biodiversity broadly includes three different but closely related aspects. They are genetic, species and ecosystem level diversities 1) Genetic diversity refers to the variations of genes within species 2) Species diversity refers to variety of species within a region 3) In eco-system diversity, there may exists different land forms each of which supports different but specific vegetation.

The well being and survival of human beings are dependent on millions of species of plants and microbes. These includes species and varieties of crops, livestock and wild life. Biological diversity is part of our daily lives and livelihood and constitutes resources upon which families, communities, nations and future generations depends. It has numerous values in agriculture, medicines, food and industry. Biodiversity maintains ecological balance and evolutionary processes and has spiritual, cultural, aesthetic and recreational values. Conservation and sustainable use of biodiversity is engrained in the Indian ethics and culture. Even to day millions of people derive their daily sustenance from forests, rivers, grasslands and seas. [12]

Biodiversity has currently emerged as an issue of global concern. The world bodies concerning environment have now come forward in an organized way to address the issue relating to biodiversity as there has been increasing threat and pressure on the biosphere. In India also, there has been a growing concern among the people on the environmental problems and issues including biodiversity during the recent years. The rapid loss of biological resources experienced in different parts of the country resulting from overuse and misuse in some cases has prompted the people and government machineries to do something positives for their conservation and sustainability. [13] A wide variety of measures can be used to conserve biodiversity including both in situ and ex situ conservation methods.

Biodiversity of Shirui Kashong
Flora Diversity

Shirui Kashong was declared as a major hot spots since the discovery of Shirui Lily which is locally known as Shirui Timrawon, Lilium Macklinae. In 1946, Mr. Kingdom ward came to Manipur on behalf of the New York botanical Society and made a sensational discovery of the famous Shirui Lily (Timrawon) which bagged the prestigious merit prize of the 1948 Royal Horticulture Society. He came along with his wife Jean Macklin and they halted at Ukhrul in a building which they called "Cobwebs Cottage". The botanical name of Shirui Timrawon (Lily) is called Lilium Macklinae Sealy which is named after his wife's name Macklin. It is a seasonal flower and its peak season of blooming is from May 15 to June 6th . The height of the plant is between 1 to 3 ft. and 1 to 9 flowers per plant. In former years one could see even upto 12 flowers per plant. The lily is bluish Pink in colour. Its beauty lies in its bell shape petals in bowing down position like a modest girl. It is a rare and endemic flower grown only on the Shirui Peak in the World. [14] The Lily grows best in partial shade with abundant humus and in open gritty soil with chromium, sunny slopes and adequate wind speed throughout the year.

Fig. 2
Shirui Lily

The habitat of endemic Shirui lily is threatened due to intensive tourists activities which are especially organized during the peak season of flowering. The dumping of waste, plastics, plucking of flowers and uprooting has threatened the sustenance of the species. The lily existence is also endangered by the invasion of Machun which is a kind of miniature bamboo species growing profusely in Shirui Kashong habitat. The dwindling growth of Shirui lily is also the cause of climate change. The State Forest Department as well as Non-Governmental organizations are working hard to save and conserve the habitat of this rare endemic species from extinction. The State Forest Department of Manipur with some financial assistance from the Central Government has been taking up some local support measures through providing awareness programme and employing five local volunteers to look after and protect Shirui Lily.

They check the tourists activities during the trek, which is mainly during the flowering months. The Mungleng Vathei Hill Development Society (MVHDS) has volunteered checking people's belonging all throughout the trekking route. Volunteers imposed fine on anyone who plucked lily from the habitat. Pits are dug along the trekking route for use as dustbin and later collected by NGO members. Fencing around the main lily area has been put up for protection. Awareness campaigns and programmes are being conducted every year. [15]

The uniqueness of Shirui Kashong is blooming of various kinds of flowers in succession throughout the year. Other flowering plants besides Shirui lily are Iris species grown on the peaks of Shirui

Kashong are: 1) Kaem feri 2) Kumaonensis 3) Milesii 4) Wattii. Not less than 150 herbaceous flowering plants including rare orchids of

various hues and crimson red rhododendrons locally known as kokliwon blooms with the advent of spring time on the grassy slopes of Shirui Kashong. In between the second and third peaks under mass clad seven rhododendron species including white variety are found viz–arboretum, johnstoneanum lindleyi, Macabeanum, Manipur sensis, triflorum vaccinioides and various multicoloured flowering annuals littered the ground in profusions. The rare white rhododendrons thrive at high altitudes of Phangrei (a part of Shirui range) are a riot of colours of rhododendrons and Bowhineas blooming in succession. [16]

Fig.3 Summer Flower

Horamwon another extraordinary feature of Shirui Kashong peak is the blooming of thousands of the shadeless white flowers locally known as Horamwon (snow flower) which cover the peak. The Horamwon is also popularly called summer flower because it blooms from the beginning of June to July. Horamwon in fact is not a big blooming flower. It is about 2cm only but numerous. It spreads over an area of about 2 sq.km.

Fig. 4
Rhododendr
on

Some of the most spectacular and representatives wild roses are growing in the mountain peaks are Rosa gigantea, Involucrata, Longicuspis, Sericea etc. Epiphytic ferns, tree ferns, wild azaleas of several kinds of orchids are also common and more than 5 different species of oak trees viz- Querous fenistrata, Q. fritfithii, Q. Lamellose, Q. Xylocarpa are also grown.

Shirui Kashong also harbours 150 species of orchids, 20 species of bamboo, 10 species of zingiberales and more than 400 species of ethnomedicinal plants, like Taxa baccata (cancer treatment plant) Thylic trum, Paris Poriphyla, Penase ginseng, Pseudo ginseng etc. are found. Further explorations are required to document more plants wealth from Shirui Kashong range. Some endangered and endemic plants are lilium maekliniae sealy (Shirui lily) L. clavidii Duch, Vaccinium, vaccinium manipurens, Agapetes manni Henesl, A. borii Airy Shaw, Rhododendron jhonstoneanum and many other species of angiosperms etc.

Faunal Diversity of Shirui Kashong

Apart from rich diversity in flora, Shirui Kashong is rich in faunal diversity. It is indeed a small Noah's ark hidden in the extreme Indo-Myanmar border where rare species of flora and fauna are preserved but nowadays many rich endemic species are near extinction due to climate change and deforestation. Its also observe that mostly, mammals and birds are explored while reptiles, amphibians, insects and other animals and birds are less explored. As per the report of Government Forests Department of Manipur, Scientists, NGOs and villagers, the following faunal diversities found along the Shirui Kashong range are Hoolock gibbon, Himalayan Black Bear, leopard, Barking deer, sambar, jackal, Migratory Indian elephant along Indo-Myanmar, Pangolin, wild boar, jungle cat, Flying squirrel, Martens, clouded leopard, Golden cat, Shirui Tiger, slow Loris, Hog badger, Antelop(serao), Stump tailed macaque, Stump Bisen, Otter, Wild dog, Gaur(Bos fromtalis Lamb), Porcupine(serao), salamander etc. Birds – jungle fowl(tharik), Parakeet, Mrs. Hume barred backed Pheasant, Blyths tragopan(vavao), Horn Bills, hawk, Koel (sampheirok) Cuckoo(koktui), Shiri (migratory bird from Siberia), Green Pea Fowl, Greayter spotted Eagle, spot billed Pelican, Eye-browned thrush. Amphibian – lengwa (tylototriton verucosus Anderson). Reptiles – Python, Cobra etc. [17]

There are still more yet to explore some of the species found on this mystic mountain ranges and also identify the vulnerable endemic species which are in near extinction. Unfortunately a great number of wild animals have extinct and the number decreased greatly due to indiscriminate hunting of games with rapid deforestation. Shirui shiri birds will be caught in great numbers which are caught by using a sticky paste called nei in Tangkhul. The taste of the bird either fresh or dried one is extremely tasty. Till last years many wild animals meat, fresh and dry meat of all kinds are sold in Ukhrul bazaar along with varieties of bird. Now selling of such jungle fowls and animal are banned. They did not even spare killing big python for extracting gall bladder for medicinal use. Even python teeths are used for healing tooth ache. The writer acute tooth ache was cured after applying two python teeth smear with wild boar bitter gall bladder. The messages of conservation of wildlife are yet to reach the interior villages. If we go to the interior border villages, the villager' will entertain the guests with the best indigenous brewed rice beer or fruit wine with any kind of wild animals and fowls.

To promote in situ conservation the Government of Manipur has proposed to declare 100 sq.km. of Shirui Kashung as national park since 25-11-1982. The proposed and settlement proceeding is not yet completed as the greater portion of the area falls under private land. As per the report of The Sangai Express 24th April 2014, though Shirui village has a huge chunk of forest land, almost 90% of the forest land belongs to private individual owners. The village headman of Shirui village W. Luiram said that in spite of the village council resolution to preserve the forest and to ban trading in forests production for ensuring better environment, the villagers lack cooperation. The village headmen also reiterated that stopping forests products is beyond his authority as they rely on the forest for fodder, timber and wood for fuel. The headman also informed that a certain villager leased his forest land to the BRTF in 2011 on monthly payment of Rs 15,000 till date for extraction of fire wood and the village authority has no power to stop him. Another area of concern raised by the villagers is the extinction of wild animals from the area due to excessive deforestation activities. "Sangh an elderly villager said that the forests area was once home to many wild animals and were frequently sighted before it was deforested. He said that chirping sound of Tragoban bird at Kashong Shongra is a thing that exists only in his memory."

Until the construction of a PMGSY road connecting Shirui to Mapum area, the tropical virgin main forest of Shirui remained unexplored and inaccessible. Once the timber merchants made an inroad into the forest they started exploring the forest and visibly the ones dense forest become sparse every passing season. Even the volume of river water flowing out from this mountains has receded drastically and due to this Ukhrul town populace is facing acute water crisis. As the villagers rampantly harvest forest products to meet their own domestic needs and for their sustenance without the slightest caring about the effects for the future, the authority concern has to act swiftly to save the rich bio diversity of Shirui Kashong[18]. People should be sensitize for the conservation of the forest. It is suggested that the whole range of Shirui Kashong hills should be declared as world heritage. Proposed Shirui National Park should be implemented at the earliest so as to safeguard the natural habitat. In situ and ex situ conservation should be promoted to safe the threatened endemic species before it is too late. In situ conservation pertains to conserving animals and plants in their natural habitat. Effective in situ conservation includes legal protection of endangered species and the establishment of protected area to conserve individual species and habitat. Ex situ conservation involves the cultivation of raw plants, rearing of threatened animals outside of their natural habitat and also herding of plant and animal species in botanical and zoological gardens and arboretums or reserve them in the form of seeds in seed bank (gene bank) or some other suitable farms by means of tissue culture and animal species which have become more or less extinct in the wild but they are being conserved in gardens or zoos. [19] These two methods of conservation can be successfully implemented for the conservation of Shirui Kashong rich biodiversity. It is also suggested to open life science research institute for undergoing more intense research work for further discovery and preservation.

Conclusion

The villagers of Shirui village who are solely dependent on forests resources should be given an alternative sustainable means of livelihood by conserving biological diversity which constitute an essential aspect of sustainable development. Sustainable use of biodiversity is a key component of sustainable social and economic development. According to commission on environmental and development (WEED) known as Brundtland Commission Report 1987, sustainable development is defined as meeting the needs of the present generations without compromising the needs of future generations". [20] Development is the process by which people meet their needs and values of all interest groups not only of the present day but of future also by conserving natural resources and diversity of life, it becomes sustainable. The goals of sustainable development are not merely the development of all human beings but that of all other species. Everybody has to realize that this planet of ours is the only known abode of life and that we have not inherited this from our fore fathers but taken it on loan from the future generations to be returned to them intact.[21] It is also suggested that government should give same alternative means of livelihood suited to the people and region so as to conserve and bring sustainable development.

References:

[1] Wildlife Biodiversity Conservation (2008), Editor: Mallapuriddi Vikram Reddy Published by – Naya Publishing House - Delhi. Article by B. Gopichand, Mizoram.

[2] Herbal Medicine of Manipur –A colour Encyclopedia (2003), H.B. Singh, R.S. Singh, I.S. Sandhu, Naya Publishing House Delhi.

[3] Kamei Gangmumei – Genesis of the Ethnoses of Nagas and Kuki-chin, Naga Students Federation (1993).

[4] G.K. Ghosh – Tribals and their culture Manipur and Nagaland vol.3, Ashis Publishing House, New Delhi – 1986.

[5] R. Muivah – TBL Centenary celebration – 1996.

[6] M. Horam – Naga Old Ways New Trends, Cosmo Pub. New Delhi, 1998. Aja Daily Nov. 16 – 1995.

[8] G.K. Ghosh – Tribal and Their Culture Manipur and Ngaland. Vol. 3. Ashis Pub. House New Delhi – 1992

[9] Wahenbam Ibohal Singh – The Histiry of Manipur (an early period) Kishori Devi Imphal 1986.

[10] Wungmareo Shaiza – T.B.L. Centenary Celebration 1996.

[11] K.C. Agrawal – Global Biodiversity – Conservation, Indigenous Rights and Biopiracy, Nidhi Publishers (India – 2002)

[12] Dr. M.P. Singh FMA, Dr. Bijay S. Singh, Ph. D, Miss Soma Dey, Conservation of Biodiversity and Natural Resources, Naya Publisher House Delhi – 2004.

[13] A.K. Bhagabati, MC Kalita, S. Baruah, Biodiversity of Assam – Status Strategy and Action for Conservation EBH. Publishers – Guwahati 2006.

[14] Ramnganing Op.cit Page 12.

[15] Subhasis Panda – Paper presented in seventh Biennial conference – Indian Society for Ecological Economics (INSEE) Global change, Ecosystems sustainability Dec. 4-8-2013 – Tezpur University.

[16] Ramnganing Op.cit Page 12

[17] Forest Department, Manipur, Wild Life Wing Manipur – Wild Life Protected areas in Manipur.

[18] The Sangai Express 24th April 2014

[19] K.C. Agnawal Op.cit Page 216

[20] Jwitesh Kumar, Debendra Kumar Das – Environmental Economics and Development Page 216 Deep & Deep Publication North Delhi – 2008

[21] Ibid Page 89